I0130068

Close to Death, Closer to God

. . . .

True Stories of a
Spiritual Awakening

MERYL YVONNE

TURNING
STONE
PRESS

First published in 2013 by
Turning Stone Press, an imprint of
Red Wheel/Weiser, LLC
With offices at:
665 Third Street, Suite 400
San Francisco, CA 94107
www.redwheelweiser.com

Copyright © 2014 by Meryl Yvonne Crump

All rights reserved. No part of this publication may be reproduced or transmitted in any form or by any means, electronic
or mechanical, including photocopying, recording, or by any
information storage and retrieval system, without permission
in writing from Red Wheel/Weiser, LLC. Reviewers may quote
brief passages.

The names of some people and animals have been changed to
protect privacy.

ISBN: 978-1-61852-086-9

Cover design by Jim Warner
Cover image: Aaron Brown

Printed in the United States of America
10 9 8 7 6 5 4 3 2 1

Mo aku mokopuna (For my grandchildren)

Ngapene, Koroheke, Rahiri, Rachel, Whakarongotai,
Mata'afa, Tihe, Georjah, Rika, Faith, Moana, Lefu,
Tu Te Kiha, Eshay, Morehu, Vayton, and Nadia and
all those waiting to come.

Be courageous as you paddle your own waka.
You are not born alone, to then follow the crowd.

Do not sacrifice your innate creativity for a safe option
or pressure from society's expectations. Your difference is
your greatness. Within life's risks lie your lessons.

Tread gently on the planet and show respect for Mother
Earth and all living creatures. Like you, they too are God.

Discipline your thoughts, emotions, and speech to those
of love and forgiveness. To harbor judgment and
resentment and to blaspheme is to block your light
and disease your body.

Be aware that drugs and alcohol are a back door to heaven
and will not bring you the joy and bliss of the real thing.

Be grateful for your embodiment. It is a privilege to be
here no matter how challenging your journey. Do not
waste your life through idleness and indifference.

Find extra time to joyously care for the old and the very young. Never lose sight of their great "being" or your responsibility to be a kind caregiver. The youth require your guidance.

Find time to go within and radiate your light to those in need. This practice will expand your spiritual awakening while healing others.

Listen to the ancient karakia (prayers) of your tupena (elders) to know truth.

Face your own death or ascension with the excitement of a new journey without need of anyone or anything. You will leave alone.

Know that you are forever blessed.

Contents

Acknowledgments

When I was six years old my teacher Miss Kerridge indulged my desire to write stories with copious pages of text and by giving me four gold stars.

Also at six years old, my sisters Debbie and Irene enjoyed my made up stories at bedtime which gave me the belief that I could "spin a yarn."

My forever partner Manu Neho for her unwavering support.

Note from the Author

The Word "God"

There are literally hundreds of names for the word God. The Hebrew letters YHWH represent the name of God. Some say it cannot or should not be pronounced and that the letters derive from the Hebrew verb "to be." This stems from the Biblical teaching, "Thou shalt not take the name of the Lord thy God in vain." (Exodus 20:7, one of the Ten Commandments)

The Jewish tradition is not to speak the sacred name at all. They instead say "Adonai" (my lord) and only during prayer. Many Jews refer to God as "Hashem" (the name) (Leviticus 24:11).

The early Christian writer Clement of Alexandria in the second century transliterated the letters YHWH as the Greek word iaoue, pronounced "Yaweh" in English.

The Indian text "Jaap Sahib" by Guru Gobind Singh contains 950 names for God.

There is "ilah"(Arabic), "Elah" (Biblical Aramaic), "ehyeh" (ancient Hebrew meaning "it will be"/"I AM"), "El" (mighty strength, power), or "Eloah" (the feminine noun meaning Goddess from the Book of Job) plus "im" (masculine suffix) to make "Elohim," the Hebrew word indicating a plurality of both masculine and feminine essences in a singular identity.

In my writings, I name this balance of masculine and feminine energy "Father/Mother God." Other names I use are "The Source," "Supreme Being," " I AM Presence," "God force," "that which has always been," or "God."

Know that they all mean the source of all being where everything else derives existence from. All are *IN* and *OF* the only *ONE*.

"The source and foundation of all possibility of utterance, and this is beyond all definite descriptions." (As revealed in the Tanakh.)

Words will always be limited and seem inadequate. Some people will have an immediate negative reaction to the word "God," perhaps due to a past experiences in a religious school or group, or being taught that "he" is a punishing God. I ask that when you read the word "God," know the true meaning and use whichever term you can be at peace with.

In the book of Exodus, God commands Moses to tell the people that "I AM" sent him. In the Mosaic tradition, this is still revered as one of the most important names for God.

Moses said to God, "Suppose I go to the Israelites and say to them, 'The God of your fathers has sent me to you,' and they ask me, 'What is his name?' Then what shall I tell them?"

God said to Moses, "I AM who I am. This is what you are to say to the Israelites: 'I AM has sent me to you.'" God also said to Moses, "Say to the Israelites: 'The Lord, the God of your fathers—the God of Abraham, the God of Isaac and the God of Jacob—has sent me to you.' This is my name forever, the name you shall call me from generation to generation." (Exodus 3:13-15)

Ehyeh-Asher-Ehyeh, I AM that I AM (or will be on going).

Close to Death, Closer to God

Preface

Thirty-thousand American citizens commit suicide every year. The elderly age group makes up the largest number of suicides, yet it is only the eleventh-most common cause of death. For teenagers, there are fewer numbers, however it is the fifth-most common cause of death. Males make up the highest numbers in both groups, with adult suicides more likely to be well planned, often involving a firearm. In the youth group, for every suicide there are one hundred attempts at suicide, which depicts a more spontaneous action of desperation, often a call for help.

In a country as small as New Zealand (4 million total population), we have approximately 550 deaths to suicide every year, with the highest portion being retired older male adults and Maori/Pacific Island male youths. This latter group increased by 40 percent in 2012.

With $62 million per annum being spent on youth suicide and youth mental health programs, the figures do not decrease, so it is clear that we are just scratching the surface of this global problem.

There are more obvious reasons for suicide in our elderly; a sense that their life is over, intolerable illness and associated pain, or the loss of a life partner, leading to depression and loneliness.

Why are the statistics so high for youth suicide and suicide attempts? This age group is considerably more likely to have their health and a future to look forward to, involving career and family. It is a time of tremendous possibility, but can also be a time fraught with stress and worry. There is pressure to fit in socially, to perform academically, and to act responsibly. Adolescence is also a time of sexual identity and relationships that are severely affected by childhood sexual abuse, which sadly continues to increase (and that is only the cases we know about). There is a need for independence that often conflicts with the rules and expectations set by others. The likelihood of suicidal thoughts is 95 percent higher when using drugs and alcohol.

What is common to all suicides is the feeling of utter hopelessness; a life without purpose or reason to live. There are many community groups and churches that go to great effort to assist and entertain the elderly and create youth groups that can give teenagers a sense of family and belonging, but on the whole our societies are bereft of spiritual guidance and truth. This is of no fault to those offering it; it is more to do with what is now a long history of spiritual disconnection. People have rebelled against the Christian teachings of an oppressive, judgmental God, which has left a gaping hole of nothingness for many generations of youth, including those that are now becoming the elderly. Without spiritual truth, there is no sense of future, for there is no connection to the unlimited potential of the great I AM presence—that which we call God, that which is life everlasting.

- A small child with a vacant, daydreaming face has just "popped out" as his way of getting closer to his I AM presence; closer to God.

- The spiritual student experiencing deep meditation is closer to God.

- The grandparent who laughs with the child is closer to God.

- The woman who cares for the animals and respects nature is closer to God.

- The writer, composer, and dancer are closer to God.

- The man who loves the quietude of fishing as he watches the sun rise is closer to God.

- The businesswoman that has one more glass of wine, as her muscles relax after a hectic day, is closer to God.

- The young man that jogs one more mile until his endorphins break through like a hot summer's day is closer to God.

- The couple that reaches orgasmic heights is closer to God.

- The sports person in the exaltation of winning gold is closer to God.

- The businessman who enthusiastically clinches the million-dollar deal is closer to God.

- The taste of exquisite food is closer to God.

- The outdoor enthusiast hurtling down the rapids or leaping from an airplane is closer to God.

- The methamphetamine addict that feels unstop-pable energy and power is closer to God, and in the days of exhaustion that follow, when he would rather die, he still yearns to be closer to God.

Whether we are conscious of our desire for greater spiritual connection or not, we all have our ways of finding light-relief, love, and bliss, all of which are our essence—that which is God. We have an innate knowingness, a dim, dark memory that our ability to feel love and our state of real joy is who we *really* are, so we will pursue whatever connects us to that feeling. The bliss of floating free of the body in deep meditation, using drugs and alcohol or the "high" of winning, all seek a similar spiritual bliss, however those that are achieved from an external source are fleeting and require repeating to maintain any sense of ongoing satisfaction. I fondly call them "the back door to heaven." They are the windows from which we observe "heaven" and touch on bliss, which ceases as soon as life throws us another curveball that brings up feelings of grief, anger, resentment, or worry.

The only connection to God that is enduring, that overlaps all other aspects of our life, is our journey within. To experience true heaven on Earth is to stay conscious while in deep relaxation as the brainwave pattern changes from Beta (active) to Alpha (deep relaxation) to Theta (conscious spiritual state) before Delta (deep sleep). The *conscious spiritual state* is a place of bliss that is our essence, our enlightenment to God, our true nature. Without the practice of deep meditation, Theta is a momentary state just before sleep. To experience this state consciously is the *journey within*. It is referred to as enlightenment because it is the awakening to the self, the I AM, that which has always been.

An open heart is the bridge for the spiritual being to be fully present in physical form. It washes clean the etheric and emotional energy fields to heal past hurts and trauma. The higher-frequency energy we then access bubbles like a river of joy, which when combined with lofty thoughts is a power that can manifest abundance in this world effortlessly.

Our insistence on closing our heart through thoughts of hatred, resentment, or judgment is our way of avoiding our own feelings of hurt and trauma.

To die is to return to a higher frequency of spirit and be closer to God until another physical incarnation is required, so even death or suicide is but a fleeting visit, closer to God.

Our *mission*, should we choose to accept it, is to live in physical form AS God. All loving, all light, all giving in every thought, action, and deed. That is what the great teachers came to show us, to love at all times is to live as our I AM presence, to fully awaken.

Jesus said: "But I say unto you. Love thine enemies, bless them that curse you, do good to them that hate you and pray for them which despitefully use you and perse-cute you." (Matthew 5:44)

"Father forgive them, for they know not what they do." (Luke 23:34)

"Love one another as I have loved you." (John 13:34)

Suicide is as much a *spiritual* problem as it is a social problem within our communities. Teenagers in particular have many questions about who and what is God and why are we here. The elderly want to know why should I stay and where am I going.

My motivation for writing my stories with the les-sons I have learned is to provide answers to some of these questions, activate enthusiasm for the personal spiritual journey within, and especially to show our youth that it is through their mistakes that they learn. These are not times to give up, but times to dig deep within, to find your power and inner strength to face life's challenges.

Kia kaha (be strong).

Do not be overwhelmed, blame others, or remain a victim in your life. Instead, find a hunger for spiritual wakening until you know that you are a part of the whole; that you matter personally as much as we all matter collectively. You are not alone, but a part of all physical matter, here to co-create with God through your ability to love and to know the truth about the great being that you are: your mighty I AM presence.

∼

"Know the truth and the truth shall set you free." (John 8:32)

"I AM the illuminating, revealing presence. I AM the wisdom, the perception and the power that brings everything before me that I might see and understand.

Through my I AM presence, I compel everything I need to know, to be revealed to me." ("I Am Discourses, Volume 3," St. Germain)

1

Just Made It: 3 Years Old

Teaching: Fear

My craft is accelerating rapidly and arcs into a night sky. As it turns, my window shows the deep ochre/ orange, grey of a revolving planet. She is one huge solid mass and very close. Her massive bulk with cratered surface is shrinking before my eyes as my ship increases speed, leaping through space.

With no warning, the planet explodes into every direction. An immense fireball lights up the sky, red and orange as far as I can see. Great boulders in flames spew dramatically into a night sky, traveling many miles into space. Like a shockwave I experience absolute, paralyzing fear. The surge of adrenaline and my thumping heart bring an overwhelming nausea to the pit of my stomach and I want to wretch.

I am three years old. My chest heaves as I gasp and throw off my blankets. Pulse thundering, my body stiff and clammy with sweat. It lasts mere moments as I remind myself, 'It is okay. It is only *the dream.*'

It happens every night, exactly the same with the fear of being caught in the flames, not knowing if I will live or die, and then the hollow grief for the planet's inhabitants. I lie awake in awe of the fiery spectacle.

I am in a small flying craft: slim line, chic, and technologically far superior to anything on Earth. It has a large concave rear window causing light rays to diverge, which propels the craft soundlessly at magnificent speed. I am not alone. There is a small team of people with me: three in the middle section strapped behind wide red belts, silently concerned, and two more in front of the control panel talking quietly and flicking switches. I feel a deep tiredness in my bones as I sink back into my body-hugging seat at the rear of the craft, and elevate my padded space boots to alleviate the tension in my calf muscles.

We walked many, many miles in a searing hot, dry landscape before unveiling the invisibility beam that surrounded our craft. A part of me feels joy to finally be leaving this loveless planet, raped of her beauty and barren of nature devas, but the overwhelming feeling is of sadness that we did all we could, but it was too little too late. We had failed and had abandoned our mission.

I gaze into a sea of twinkling stars and the soundless rotation of chiseled chunks of space matter as we travel through the multiverse. I am enjoying the sudden thrust of speed as we head for the wormhole that will take us to our next destination. My last images are of red, orange, and brilliant gold. Blazing fire is all around us as our craft hurtles itself out of the flames. Movement is instant. As fast as blinking, we zip faster than the speed of light, as smooth as silk, ppeee . . .uu . . . and we are gone into space through the blur of starlight.

I sit silently and fight to regain my breath. I am thirty-five years old with short black hair in a cream and turquoise leather-type suit, streamlined like my craft. I look at my other crew members. No one speaks or looks at another as we all contemplate leaving our last destination.

It is the panic locked in my small out-stretched stiffened legs and my inability to breathe that wakes me. My first realization is always the same.

"Wow, we just made it."

I feel intense relief as my pulse begins to slow.

People, on the whole, do not have the connection into the subconscious to be able to visit specific memory from another incarnation and bring it through to this time zone. It helps to be uncluttered like a child. A three-year-old child in a dream state.

The *dream* was with me for what seemed a very long time in my short life. It stopped when I was five years old—like switching off a light, it just never came back. I used to wonder as I grew older why it had to be so repetitive when I had survived? Why was it such a prominent memory?

I had never before sighted images of space, planets, or flying ships. It was 1963. We did not even have a television, let alone computer games or vast collections of images on YouTube or other social media sites. We were not allowed comic strip books, so the images in my mind were limited to sketches of bunny rabbits from the Beatrix Potter Peter Rabbit series, which I visited regularly at the bottom of my cereal bowl.

The images in my *dream*, I have never seen on planet Earth as they are not from Earth, yet everything is totally familiar to me. There is no doubt in my mind as a small child that the woman in the spacesuit is me and I was there. By the time I am five years old, it is very clear to me that I have lived many lives.

I was twenty-five years old before further explanation was given to me. Robert and Helena, spiritual teachers from America, said that they received guidance to travel to New Zealand to "find a young woman that would be a significant healing force in the South Pacific." They were to *awaken* my innate talent as a Master Healer and get me working.

I gave this information little heed at the time, but realized after many years running my own private healing clinics in New Zealand and Australia, that everything they reminded me of was accurate in its ability to achieve results. I would watch them work and every hair on the back of my neck would stand to attention as waves of familiarity would wash over me with a nostalgic feeling of "coming home."

"You *walked into* your body when it was three years old. The original host agreed to prepare it for you so that you did not have to go through the fetal and infant stages. You slipped in after a severe bump on the head when unconscious for but a moment.

"You are what we call a time traveler," Robert said matter of factly.

"You travel between universes to planets in transition that require assistance. Because you arrived at the age of three, your most significant memory of your last mission stayed with you, until it eventually blurred by the time you were five years old and was consumed by the density of Earth's three-dimensional energy."

"Ooo . . . kay . . . right-o," I thought skeptically.

This information was coming from a man with a bald head, bulbous eyes, and protruding ears, who looked like he had just arrived from Mars. I wanted to believe him, for this was the first thing ever said to me that helped make any sense of my memory. I decided not to contemplate it further and to simply get on with the work. My passion was my truth. I had huge enthusiasm and pleasure in seeing people reconnect to their greater energy flow, watching them as they would rise like a phoenix from the ashes toward their true potential. Robert and Helena showed me how past emotion held on to memories that cluttered the energy field. They would surface and permanently dissipate, leaving the main chakras (energy wheels) open and spinning, bringing with them new vitality and joy. People became more open and real before my eyes, and I could see that all their pain, control, arrogance, anger, and grief was the illusion—the protection they stood behind. Once people were still and vulnerable, I could see God. All light, all love, all joy, and it was in each of us. After the rage, then the tears, there was only laughter. More and more unstoppable laughter. My clients have gone on to change people's lives through film, documentaries, books, performance, politics, corporations, and parenthood to name a few, throughout the South Pacific and beyond.

So why time travel to Earth? What is the transition Earth is experiencing?

Planets themselves evolve as we do. The people of Earth have not lived in their true light for many thousands of years and require great healing so that the planet herself can progress to a higher fifth-dimensional frequency of love and peace.

Earth took on many planetary orphans. These are beings whose planets have gone on to evolve into a higher frequency without them. These beings were too shrouded in darkness and negativity to evolve with their planets, as they were not ready for higher frequencies generated by love. Earth beings at that time were luminous in their light and lived without disease for two thousand years. They mastered three-dimensional existence in no more than seven incarnations before ascending into the fifth-dimensional energy of pure love. This was known as the *normal progression of a soul through physical matter*.

With great compassion, the people of Earth offered their services to the orphans so that they could continue to evolve. They believed they would lift these lost souls out of their darkness. There was much debate and many people on Earth opposed this decision. As feared, Earth was overwhelmed by the extent of the dark behavior devoid of love, which entangled her people into destructive emotions, which ultimately set them back in their own evolution many thousands of years. At one stage, there was indecision as to whether Earth and her people could ever be raised back to their frequency of magnificence.

Thousands of Light workers from other dimensions have offered their time and energy tirelessly to come to Earth's aid and assist humanity back to awareness. They have endured great suffering to be present in such density to assist the people of Earth back to their rightful place of awakened awareness. Many sensitive beings have been unable to sustain the pain of being amidst the hatred, negativity, and atrocious behavior born out of disconnected hearts. They have abandoned their mission by departing early through accidents or disease. Others have succumbed to chronic illness often due to immune system failure or have required drugs and alcohol to regularly exit the body for some light relief. There is good news however. The shift back to the light of love has been successful and continued spiritual progress is now assured. As more people awaken with unhindered energy flow, great joy accompanies them. Over the next one thousand years, every being on planet Earth will awaken to their higher frequency, which will catapult the Earth herself into fifth-dimensional frequency. We will then truly see "Heaven on Earth" whereby people can manifest with ease. This will put an end to greed, corruption, poverty, starvation, disease, and disasters from adverse weather conditions.

There have been "seers" like Nostradamus who predicted one thousand years of peace for planet Earth. All the preparation from all the Light workers has tipped the balance positively toward this prophecy and the thousand years has begun, whereby every man, woman, and child will awaken to know their true divine I AM presence.

So are we catching this ride or not? We either join Earth in paradise in a new sea of love or we hold on to our old patterns of control, manipulation, revenge, and hatred. Some will fight to the death. Rest assured, death will again be sweet relief though temporary. There will no longer be an invitation to attend this Earthly learning institution in three-dimensional energy. Earth will move on in her evolution, and a new "university" is forming in the third dimension. This planet has already been born into our solar system.

The people from the planet in the dream went so far in their imbalance that they destroyed their host. As their planet explodes and I experience fear for my own safety, I have no access to my innate knowingness while in this state. My body stiffens and my heart and adrenal systems work harder. Fear is so powerful and so all-consuming that it has the ability to freeze my body completely. My blood pressure and perspiration rates increase, and I gasp for breath. The emotions are so intense that something "has to give" into the acceptance of *not knowing if I will live or die*. The repetitiveness of the dream gives me the opportunity to practice this over and over again. By the age of five years old, I have mastered how to be the observer of the horror. I learn how to enter a space in my mind whereby I can stay present without emotional attachment. I observe the events dispassionately while waking peacefully, accepting what is happening without fear. The memory never changes, but I change. I still face the split second when I have no knowledge as to whether I will live or die, which remains as real and uncertain as the first time the memory surfaced, but I can wake without any emotion. In this process of surrender, a sea of bliss closely follows within a frequency of light where fear does not exist.

In all my work with previous trauma, the events that clutter the etheric energy field from previous incarnations are usually locked into the field at the time of sudden death. That is, there was no time to process and accept the event or forgive the cause of death. My repetitive memory has a satisfactory ending, so why does it keep repeating from my subconscious?

Memory is stored by emotion. The *fear of death* was so all consuming that it completely overlapped my next bodily incarnation. If it had happened once or twice, I might call it a dream. Night after night for two years, it is called a memory. At three years old, I have the ability to bring some of the unconscious through the veil to conscious awareness. This is early training for my lifetime of work.

In the process of remembering, I know that reincarnation exists, as does life on other planets. There are billions of suns and billions of galaxies that support life.

I know that our emotional field goes with us when we are away from our body and that the clutter of unresolved undesirable emotion is cumulative and creates spiritual wounds in the energy field. These wounds cannot be healed until they are released via memory, as an impure emotion that passes through the physical form. This can be immediate with a gurgle of the intestines and a jerk of the limbs or painstakingly slow as old patterns repeat themselves in our relationships with others.

The emotion will look for a vent over and over again until you transmute it into a different form.

This is why we see familial patterns in relationships, work, and social behavior. For example, if your issue is anger or the abused victim, the events that create those emotions will continue to follow you around through every aspect of your life until they are resolved. The most common reason for lack of resolution is the inability to remember the old experience and bring it into conscious awareness. The being incarnates again with no memory of the past or becomes an adult with no memory of childhood trauma.

Great compassionate beings wishing to assist Earth could see that human beings reincarnating were overwhelmed by their emotional history of victim or perpetrator and quickly became absorbed again in the negativity of those emotions. It was decided that all beings would be born with a fresh start, a blank page with no memory of the past. Though necessary, it further complicated things as people were now truly in the dark with no knowledge of the great beings they began their journey as, before ever entering third-dimensional matter! This has led to the greatest mistake made by mankind, to constantly search outside of themselves for the answers to their misery, whether it be in the form of relationships, illness, or the lack of material possessions. Alternatively, they may have joined the millions who shunned the material world to go in search of teachers so that they may attain enlightenment. Their light has always existed. It has simply been dimmed from one's conscious memory, and the more people get caught up in material, worldly drama, the less they remain in contact with the higher beings that can guide them.

Like worms, we have groveled in the dust of poverty, despair, ignorance, and self-hatred with limited knowledge of the great God force within that is all love, capable of ease and instant manifestation. Why shun the delights of material pleasure when we are one with the great God force that created them? We are here to enjoy and delight in our creations in physical form in perfect balance and knowingness of our I AM presence; not endure a life of hardship and denial while we search for something we have never lost.

Lifetime after lifetime of continued undesirable thoughts, actions, and unresolved emotional pain has reduced much of the human race to a pitiful sight of struggle, disease, and misery. Take a look in your own neighborhood. Our species is bent and lopsided in bodies aching with pain, depressed, angry, and stricken with grief, attaining fleeting happiness from relationships, food, sex, and material resources outside of themselves.

Light workers from other dimensions have offered their time and energy tirelessly to assist humanity back to awareness. The initial work has been long and hard due to layer after layer of "misqualified" energy that has jammed the etheric and emotional energy fields, separating people from their divinity and causing grave illness.

The old clutter in people's etheric fields has been clearing faster and faster as we move toward the tipping

Close to Death, Closer to God

point where all beings will instantaneously receive the benefits of greater consciousness.

Let yourself imagine a world where all political and personal decisions are made from an open heart; where the well-being spiritually, emotionally, and physically of *all* people is paramount. Those currently in power intent on personal greed at the expense and suffering of others will be given the opportunity to change and move with a loving fifth-dimensional frequency or they will leave planet Earth.

My memory showed me that my unresolved emotion was the *fear of death*. The Master teachers from the East say that this is humanity's greatest fear and it is this that stops our progression to Christ consciousness, our awakened state. We remain trapped in three-dimensional energy, a victim to the circumstances created by our limited thinking. As a child, this fear was my strongest memory and came from another time entirely. It repeated itself over and over again, until I learned to become the observer and transmute fear into acceptance, which then became bliss—the place where fear does not and cannot exist. This lesson of being *close to death* repeats itself many times in my life, each time bringing new realizations, which ultimately leads me back to my true nature, *closer to God*.

❦ 2 ❧

Running "the Gap": 11 Years Old

Teaching: Death

I never tired of watching the swirling white foam as the waves crashed into "the gap," exploding against the rock face as they turned back on each other, sucked out to sea, exposing the glint of wet, shining pebbles. As the next wave thundered in, I have a strange feeling deep in my belly, somewhere between fear and awe at the sheer power of the water. My mind wants to wander into the horror of being caught in the backward pull to no return, or body flailing, smashing into the barnacle-covered rocks with the relentless surging waves. I swiftly chastise my mind. Stop it! It is too hideous to imagine.

Thoughts return of the fisherman found floating upside-down last summer, washed from his lucky spot on the rocks. Not so lucky after all. Our hushed tones around the campfire speak of the horror, a damper to our holiday spirit, yet at the same time we are fascinated by the turn of events. The local Maori put a Rahui on the coast and we were told we could not swim for two weeks or until they found the body of his ten-year-old son.

"Come on, run!" I called to my friend Hazel. We had our fishing lines in hand and a jar of bait. It was summer. I wore shorts and a light summer t-shirt. We had not a care in the world.

Hazel's family owned a 700-acre coastal paradise in Northland where I spent most of my weekends. It wasn't all fun and games. We worked hard mustering sheep, being rouses on shearing day, or peeling endless potatoes for the shearing gang's midday roast dinner. There was the smell of lanolin oil and sheep shit in the sheds, the salt ocean breeze, and always the delectable smells wafting from the kitchen. There seemed to be an endless procession of food for hard-working men. Huge platters of scones, pikelets, and mutton sandwiches, and that was just morning tea. The steaming roast and vegetables would be served promptly at midday and us kids tucked in with the best of them. We were part of the team. A quick wash of the hands in the cow trough and with plate in hand and your bottom parked on the nearest hay bale, all was well in the world.

By the afternoon, we were free to do as we please and off we ran down to the beach and out of sight. We had a favorite fishing spot out past the headland on big, flat black rocks that would heat up in the sun. We had to steel our nerves and run through "the gap" to reach them. This involved climbing down six feet of jagged rock, leaping into "the gap," as the wave withdrew, running across the soft pebbled sand about twenty-five feet to the other side, and clambering up the rocks before the next wave came swirling in. We got cut hands and feet sometimes, which never bothered us until they stung in the salt water. If they wouldn't stop bleeding, we would use a bit of dry fiber off the harakeke (flax) plant and bandage it tight. It had to stop eventually.

We were taught to know when full tide was, for if you headed home too late "the gap" was a swirling mass of frothing white water that could not be passed. There were deaths every summer off that stretch of coast. Fisherman too close to the rock edge at high tide mainly. Swept away with a "freak wave" that appeared to come from nowhere. No one could ever survive the pounding of the waves against the rocks and often bodies were never found. There was a blow hole further around the headland near our fishing spot, the rocks worn smooth by the smashing waves that spurted thirty feet into the air. We would get as close to it as we dared, watching the retreat of the waves in horror at the thought of ever falling into that deep dark crevice.

I would get that feeling again, bordering on nausea as fear shuddered through my body.

When we were tired of casting our lines into the deep blue waters below, we would return to the beach to swim or snorkel until we shook with cold or fear after sighting a baby shark or stingray. We would return to the rocks to lie in our bikinis and the warmth from the stone would radiate through to our very bones.

We would be gone for hours. Nobody ever worried about us or came looking for us. Late into the summer twilight Hazel's mum and dad would see our two shadowy figures climbing the farm path back to the half-built farm house. I don't remember ever telling them what we had been doing. We would hang our wet bikinis on the veranda rail, lay out our kina shells to dry in tomorrow's sun, and scramble hungrily around the kitchen table.

Plates of waiting food would be lifted from the oven and there was always jelly and ice cream to follow. Bath and bed, tired out, was pretty much the routine before an early start on the farm the following morning.

One summer after our first fishing expedition of the season, we headed home across the flat rocks that led to "the gap." We discovered to our horror that it was already full of deep swirling water that did not subside as wave after wave came crashing in. We could not understand how we had got the time wrong, but resigned ourselves to returning to our fishing spot to climb the rock face to a small shelf where we would have to wait a further two hours for high tide, then six hours for the tide to turn, and at least another hour or so for the water level to retreat. It was not the first time we had had to climb to the safety of the ledge for the long wait, willing the hours to pass.

It was only 10 a.m., so we figured no one would get too worried about our absence as long as we were home by nightfall. We resigned ourselves to a long, boring afternoon, cursing our stupidity. It was lunch time and we were both hungry. We surrendered any idea we had of making pancakes for lunch with a cold lamb chop. Neither of us had packed more than a towel to combat the increasing sea breeze.

As we rounded the headland ready to climb to the shelf, I noticed that the surging waves were bigger than normal with the salt spray damp on our bare legs. I thought again, 'I know it is not full tide yet. Why are the waves so high?'

"The tide looks high, eh?" I commented to Hazel.

"Yeah, we must have read it wrong in the paper," Hazel responded without further concern.

I knew we had not misread the time for high tide as it was so important. As I gazed at the swirling sea, a particularly large wave smashed against the rock face and sprayed across the flat rocks where we normally sun-bathed. I again had an ominous feeling of unease.

We collected some dry wood, fibers, and twigs, which we carried in our beach bags up the ten feet to our rock ledge. We had nicked a couple of cigarettes and some matches and had been practicing smoking, so we were pleased to be able to light our small fire. My stomach sure wasn't going to last until 7 p.m., so we used my pocket knife to gut and scale our two small fish and cut holes in the flesh to push a stick through so we could hold them over the fire. Some time between burning sticks and charcoal, we ate soft white flesh and felt mighty proud of ourselves.

As we sat chatting, Hazel commented that the tide seemed to be coming in much higher than usual. I had done nothing *but* look at the tide, but had not wanted to alarm her. The sea was rough and was starting to splash a bit towards our ledge. High tide was midday and it was only 11 a.m. It had another hour to rise yet, and the deep green swirling water was way too close for comfort. The horror of the fisherman and his young son who was never found haunted my thoughts. Local lads had commented, "Yeah, the sharks probably got 'em."

I shuddered. "I don't like this, high tide is not for another hour yet."

Hazel, still unperturbed giggled, "Nuh, it must be high now. You must have read it wrong."

Ten minutes later the first "freak wave" lapped right over the edge and put the fire out with one dumping of icy water that splashed over our legs. Hazel screamed with fright.

"Oh God, oh God. . . . We're going to die! . . . HELP!! . . . SOMEONE PLEASE HELP US!" she screamed.

The sound of her calling was futile as it was dissipated by the wind and sucked into the depths of the ocean as soon as it was uttered. We both looked upwards with the natural instinct to get away from the rising tide, only to be confronted by a sheer rock face. There was another ledge about twelve feet further up, but how to get to it? I could see some possible foot holds and some large tree roots I would need to reach. To slip while trying could easily mean falling into the swirling water below. Should I try to climb or risk being washed off our narrow ledge? Neither option was a good one. Another wave hit the rock face just below us and sprayed our ledge with sea water.

"We have to climb higher," I stated, making my decision. I fought to control waves of panic and fear.

"I can't. I will fall. I don't want to die!" Hazel sobbed, looking wide-eyed at the crashing waves directly below us.

"We have to climb!" I repeated.

"No, I can't! It is too dangerous. We will fall." Hazel was adamant and frozen to the spot.

There seemed to be no escape. The adrenaline coursing through my body made my legs feel shaky. My mind kept searching for a solution. The one thing I was sure of was that we were in serious trouble.

I remembered how we had been gazing at the full moon from our bedroom window the night before and realized that this was what was referred to as a Spring Tide or Full Moon Tide. That, combined with the rough water after a storm at sea, the waves would definitely rise farther yet. There was no point shouting. There was no one to hear us. There was no point waving. There was no one to see us.

I remember that moment when I looked at death. Hazel's wailing became distant and quiet and my body felt light. I remembered someone having said to me once that drowning was quite a nice way to die. I remember wondering how they knew.

I wanted to be dead before my body smashed against the ragged rocks for I did not want to feel pain. I would have to make myself gulp the sea water as fast as possible. It would be okay. I knew I would return to the light and that they would be waiting for me. And who were "they"? I didn't know exactly. Lots of people, and they all love me. I did not need anyone to tell me that there was life after death. There was simply no doubt. They would all be there and I would be no more dead than the rising sun or a gentle rain. I just knew it. All panic passed and the only thought I could not bear was seeing the pain and shock my family would feel. My mother's streaming tears, my sisters' disbelief, and my father, such a protector, wishing he had been with me to find a way to fix this terrible predicament I was in. He was such a capable man. He would think of something.

I gasped, back in my body as cold water slapped against my feet. Yes, he would do something. If only we had a rope. I looked at the harakeke plant to one side of our rock ledge and remembered seeing in a museum how the Maori had plaited strong fibers from this plant to make sturdy ropes. I grabbed my pocket knife, quickly cut the long pieces of flax from the base of the plant, and stripped each piece lengthwise into three narrow strands. Hazel and I regularly plaited each other's hair, so I soon had her fully involved in making our rope. It temporarily stopped the surging panic until another wave sprayed our ledge and Hazel squealed with fright. As we completed each section of rope, we knotted them together. My fingers working as fast as possible, disappearing into a blur of tears that I seemed to have no control over.

I kept seeing my family, "I am so sorry . . . so sorry," I kept repeating silently.

I knew throughout the time it took to plait the harakeke that it was me that would have to climb the rock face. Hazel could not do it.

With the rope finally long enough, I tied one end to a protruding tree root on the side of our ledge and the other end tightly around my waist, leaving my hands and feet free for climbing. The plan was that if I slipped and fell, the rope would hold me until I clambered back to our ledge. There was no guarantee our knots would hold the force of a fall or the swirling water. I kicked off my sandshoes for fear of slipping and went barefoot. I had to reach a higher tree root to have any chance of getting to the next ledge. I asked Hazel to give me the strongest, highest leg up she could.

"You know. Just how we do it to get on top of the big horse," I said with encouragement as she wailed, "It is too dangerous! Don't leave me!"

Giving a good leg up was something Hazel knew all too well how to do, and it temporarily took her mind off impending doom. I bent my left leg backward from the knee and she cradled my knee in both hands while I prepared to push off with my right leg in a full crouch.

"One, two . . . Up!"

I pushed off with concentrated purpose and stretched as far as I could, only to miss the tree root by about three inches and slide gently back down the rock face on my belly. I was vaguely aware of pain from the graze to my stomach.

"Nearly!" I said excitedly. "Let's try again. Lift as hard as you can!"

On the next attempt I had the root firmly in the grasp of my right hand with my left foot resting partially in Hazel's hands and partially on her shoulder. I felt for the foothold I had seen earlier with my right foot and was able to push higher. Falling was simply not an option.

"Don't think about it. Don't imagine it. Look up. Look forward. You're nearly there. See yourself on the ledge. Safe. Safe."

This banter went through my mind constantly in a way that I now understand was keeping me focused on the task at hand. To allow the mind to wander was to invite failure. By now the first tree root was being used as a foothold while I grabbed at another and finally pulled myself onto the higher ledge by holding firm onto a piece of jutting rock.

I don't recall any pause to feel relief as I hurriedly untied the flax rope from around my belly and wrapped it around the jutting rock, securing it tight.

"Untie the rope at your end and tie it around your waist," I called down to her.

"I can't do it! It is too steep!" she cried.

I was acutely aware that there was no one to give Hazel the leg up that I had received and that I would have to pull her up the first part of the rock, fully reliant on our plaited rope. I had real fear for her safety, but made a point of not showing it as Hazel looked up at me with sheer terror in her eyes.

"One step at a time, eh? Just get it tied around your waist," I encouraged.

I could see the rise and fall of the swell behind her and thought that if a freak wave washed her from the shelf, I would have some chance of pulling her back. Hazel suddenly screamed as water came over the ledge and swirled around her feet. She was really crying now and pleading, "I don't want to die. HELP!!"

Again her cries were taken by the wind dipping and diving like the gulls hovering for our fish scraps. Oh, for a set of wings! There was nothing I wouldn't do to just fly home with my friend now. If birds had evolved to fly and we were the most evolved species on Earth, why couldn't we fly? I had spent hours in the past, watching the birds catching the wind drafts, soaring with wings wide through the sky or diving for fish. How I yearned to fly.

"Come on," I called. "Just like in the movies! Hold the rope and move up the rock with your feet."

I knew I had to pull her up as far as the first tree root. I prayed that our rope would hold, for I knew if it broke I would lose her. I realized in that moment just how serious the situation was. From a morning of chasing sheep through gates, a day of light-hearted chat and squealing delight at catching fish, to this life-threatening horror. My dear friend was before me, wide-eyed, frozen with fear, with a real chance of dying.

I sat down, maneuvered my feet in behind an upright section of rock, and prepared to pull. I could no longer see Hazel from this position, so I listened for her call.

I remember thinking, 'If I can't pull her up, the waves might get really high and push her up as long as the rope holds.'

As I watched the power of the swirling water, I knew in my heart that that was an unlikely possibility, and

Close to Death, Closer to God

thankfully that theory did not have to be tested. With a lot of effort, Hazel got to the first foothold and a handhold on the first tree root. When she eventually slithered over the rock edge, we cried with a mixture of exhaustion and relief.

Within twenty minutes I looked over the edge to see our lower ledge fully submerged with its first big dumping of water and my sandshoes being swept out to sea. The horror of seeing that small part of me being tossed from one surge of water to another confirmed that if we had not climbed higher, we would be dead. It was too hard to comprehend that our lives would be over.

Death is not something an eleven-year-old readily thinks about. The only dead thing I had ever seen was my mum's canary after my dad mistakenly used a lead-based oil paint for its bird cage. I remembered because she cried. I had an uncle who died and I never forgot my aunty's ashen face, torn with the shock and disbelief of his passing as she took to her bed. People always cried a lot when people they loved died. I wanted to say, "Don't be so sad. It won't be long before you see them again."

I learned that it brought little comfort as they had no proof. They wanted some sort of guarantee that I could not offer. We talked about faith at a local church group I attended. That seemed proof enough for me.

I sat for a long time in silence, huddled in my towel with the sound of the waves pounding the rocks below, quite in awe of the transient nature of our existence.

As the light faded, the unforgiving tide retreated enough for us to run "the gap."

"You're home a bit late," Hazel's dad said over his newspaper. "Have a quick bite and into bed. Big day mustering tomorrow, and I need you kids up at the top gates."

Big day. Yep, we knew about them. We never told Hazel's parents what had happened, and instead in an unusual effort not to talk about it, we told our elaborate story about cooking our fish over the fire, which we said had kept us at the beach until late. We didn't want anyone to stop us going to our fishing spot.

We didn't talk about it that night lying in our single beds with the full moon shining through the windows. It lit up the room like daylight. We processed the shock of our ordeal in our own silence until we fell asleep. From that day on, we only ever fished as the tide turned to go out.

There is nothing like imminent death to make you think about it.

I had gazed into the crashing, swirling water and come to a place where I knew it would be okay to die. I had planned how to go with minimal pain and I saw those that loved me welcoming me on the other side. There was no way my life was over, just the blink of an eye and a new beginning. How did I know that? I did not recall talking about it with anyone. When confronted with the real possibility of dying, the afterlife was very real. The thought of it all being over was just ludicrous. How did people live their life believing that at the moment of death, that was it? It just goes dark, you are no more . . . all snuffed out? I did not know where I had learned the truth. I just knew it to be so.

I grew up a lot that summer of my eleventh year. I learned that I was strong—really strong mentally, emotionally, and physically—and that all three were intrinsically linked. I learned that without mental focus, the emotions ran riot and the body could not function; that there was peace in the acceptance of death, yet at the same time I had an intense desire to live. Why was it so important to live? It was a deep survival instinct we all carry that would have us searching for a solution to survive. We would claw at life until bloodied and bruised if it meant we would live. We would bargain with life, "I will change, just let me live!"

We could be angry with life when it did not fulfill potential promises and we would wail in our grief when someone died. Why? I understood the personal grief of missing someone, but did we honestly think we would not see them again? Now that would be something to be sad about! No wonder people were afraid. How could we be sure we would ever see them again? Who could prove it to us or give us a guarantee? If I feared that my loss was permanent when I lost a loved one, then where did that leave me when I died? Now I am really frightened!

If I believe that which is my physical world is all that is real, then I cannot bear to lose my attachment to it. All of my possessions that I have worked for, all the people I love that love me, all gone into nothingness. The fear of death was the same feeling that someone had when handed a diagnosis of cancer, and the same fear that had Hazel rooted to the spot, feeling powerless as to how she was going to survive.

"I don't want to die!"

The smash and spray against the rocks. The campfire stories of yet another fisherman being sucked to his death and how no one could survive the pounding of the waves or the marauding sharks. My worst, hideous nightmare.

I knew that upon death I would no longer be with my body and thus would feel nothing. I looked right at the inky blue ocean and accepted that death would be okay.

If facing the fear of death assisted my advance from my unconscious state to my full potential as the light of God, Christ consciousness, then this experience was an important pre-adolescent initiation.

I contemplated how fear immobilized my friend as she felt sheer terror and how, when it appeared obvious that we would die, I was able to surrender to a deep faith that brought a quiet peace and realize that I was not afraid to die. The moment I accepted death, I was able to access a calm knowingness that I had a choice. I am the master of my reality and it was clear to me that I had not done what I came for and it was not my time to leave. Against inconceivable odds, I set about finding a solution to enable our survival.

I spent many years after this contemplating death and observing people's grief and fear associated with death. Later in my nursing years, I specialized in Death and Dying for seven years, assisting patients' transition from this world to the next as pain-free as possible.

I found it hard to cry at funerals and found myself speaking instead to the spirit of the one crossing over. At one such funeral, I arrived late and stood at the back of the church. It was a Catholic ceremony with the over-powering smell of burning incense as the priests swung the brass thuribles on chains. The young man had died of AIDS. A year earlier I had used burning sage when clearing the energy within his high-class apartment. He had moved in to discover old blood stains on his kitchen floor where a previous tenant had murdered his girlfriend. As I stood in the back of the church talking to the young man in spirit, I wished him a safe and adventurous journey. Suddenly I was surrounded by the unmistakable smell of sage. My friend, familiar with the sage I used in my work, whispered, "Can you smell that? Burning sage. It is him isn't it?"

The priests were definitely not burning sage. This was one way for the spirit to make itself known to two people who understood that the body was gone but he was not. Such experiences simply reinforced my knowing that death was not an end, so there was no need to fear it.

~

It is in the letting-go process that death is of any great consequence, fear is able to dissolve and the inner knowingness can arise. I then simply needed to decide that I wanted to survive. With fearlessness I am able to stay present and think rationally with my energy open and focused. This lets in more of my higher consciousness and the wise counsel that could come through me.

As I accepted death, I remembered how my body became lighter and lighter with Hazel's crying distant as a deep, peaceful trance enveloped me. Only from this "altered state" could I receive the guidance of what to do to survive. I felt free and powerful, having embraced *death* and survived.

≈ 3 ≈

My Sick Friend: 14 Years Old

Teaching: Courage

It suddenly dawned on me that I should be getting home. I stood on Pamela's front porch looking at the pouring rain as the gutter overflowed and I shuddered at the thought of driving all the way home. There was no option for staying. My life would not be worth living if my father found out that I had driven his Mini pickup truck over twenty miles on a main highway with no driver's license. I was underage and had never driven farther than the driveway at home and 5 mph in a small side street practicing gear changes with a friend's big sister. Tonight I had braved the journey to be with my friend who was unwell. All had run smoothly until the arrival of nightfall and a serious storm.

I said my goodbyes and ran to the car. Once inside, it was pitch black. The interior light did not seem to be working. I cursed as I fumbled about. I did not have a clue how to turn on the headlights and could not find the ignition. I braved another dash back to my friend Pamela's house to fetch a flashlight, and got pretty wet in the process.

Motor roaring. Headlights on. Find the lever for dim and full beam. Seat belt on. Gas, clutch, don't stall, and off I drive into the sleeting rain. The wipers are going as fast as they can and visibility is still poor as the little windshield fogs up on the inside. For the first time that night I chastise myself for my stupidity. There are no street lights this far out of town and the rain is blowing in sheets across the black tarmac under the beam of my headlights. There is a car a distance in front of me and I keep as close as possible to utilize the light from the tail lights, which makes it easier to know where I am on the road. My hands grip the steering wheel when huge trucks rock the little Mini as they thunder past in the opposite lane. I wanted to cry, but I have to hold it together.

"Watch the white line. Stay on your side of the road. Stay with the car in front. One more hill and you are on the home straight. It will be easier when you have street lights," I coax myself.

I already had a plan in my mind. Drive the car into the garage and chamois it down to dry it off and mop the water off the garage floor. If there is a little water, it will appear as nothing unusual. Dad will think I washed the car so I could have a turn at driving it about in the driveway.

Halfway up the steep hill, nearly there, and suddenly, nothing! I pump the accelerator and nothing! The motor is dead. My only thought is, 'Shit, I don't want to do a hill start.' I had not taken much time to practice them yet.

I quickly check the rearview mirror. Thankfully there are no lights behind me as I pull as far to the side of the road as possible before the car comes to a complete stop. I am still too close to the road for safety and face the difficulty of backing down the slope of the road to move further onto the grassy verge. With the heavy rain and poor backing lights it is almost impossible to see. I feel grateful for my previous practice at parallel parking. I manage to get the car off the road and leave the parking lights on to notify any passing cars. I crank the motor over and over again to no avail. It will not start.

Feeling panicky, I wonder what do I do now? Dad cannot know I have driven the car on the highway, in the night, in a storm! He will kill me. I have to get home.

It was pitch black everywhere I looked except one little light up a side road in the distance. I step out of the car and gasp as the icy sleeting rain stings my face and quickly wets my clothes. I lock the doors and head off in the torrential rain toward the direction of the light. My sandals flick mud and slide underfoot as I find the entrance to the farm. I am very grateful for Pamela's flashlight as I round bend after bend, open and close three gates, until I finally see the welcome lights of the farm house. It is about 9:30 p.m., and I look completely bedraggled, wet from head to foot with my long hair limp and saturated and clothes clinging to my skin. The woman who opens the door quickly calls for her husband. She brings me a towel and offers me a hot drink. I am seriously cold but insist that I would rather get home to a hot shower as it was not far. Her husband offers to tow me home.

The kindness and generosity of some rural folk never ceases to amaze me. It is like it is in their DNA after generations of families helping each other out. The greater the need, the more they unconditionally offer assistance.

Out in that teaming rain, the kindly farmer runs a rope to my car.

"Have you ever been towed before, luv?" he queries.

"No," I reply honestly.

"Okay," he shouts over the top of the pouring rain. "Don't brake until you see my brake lights. I will touch the brake briefly when I am about to slow or stop, then you slow down with me. Okay?"

"Yep, got it." I try to appear confident but am incredibly nervous. The last thing I want to do is damage the car. How would I explain that?

I gave the kindly farmer directions and I was soon on my way home, my eyes glued to his brake lights. It was easier than I had anticipated and it didn't seem long before we were outside my address. I had told my new-found savior to just drop me at the top of the driveway and I would run the car down to the garage. He undid his rope and I thanked him immensely.

'What would happen tomorrow morning when the car wouldn't start?' I thought.

Dad was a mechanic. He would see to it and he had no reason to link it to me.

With a bit of effort, I managed to push the Mini into the garage. I breathed a sigh of relief that my parents had not come home early. I wiped every raindrop off the car and mopped up the pools of water on the floor, showered with the water as hot as my skin could take it, and lay with huge relief cuddled under my duvet.

I did it. Phew. That was a close call and one I never wanted to repeat.

My mind flashed back to the events of the night. Going to my friend Pamela's side seemed like the most natural and normal thing to do. She had planned to visit me that night in her mum's old VW, car but had been grounded for staying out too late the night before. She had also missed a day at school with a heavy head cold and had been told by her parents to stay home and stay in bed.

"I really want to see you!" she exclaimed. "I have heaps of stuff I need to talk to you about. It's just not fair!"

Pamela blew her nose loudly and stifled a tear. At fifteen years old she had her driver's license and regularly "blatted around" in her mother's aging Beetle.

"Mum insists I stay home until I am over the flu. I am home all by myself and it is freezing. I just don't have the strength to chop wood and the heater won't go. I feel so miserable. I really want to see you!" she continued.

I did my best to console her and eventually hung up the phone bitterly disappointed that my friend was unable to visit. My parents were out at a golf function and both my sisters were staying with friends. I sat quietly for a time contemplating my options on what was shaping up to be a long, boring night in front of the tele.

Without a great deal of thought, I spontaneously leapt to my feet, grabbed my jersey, and went to the garage. Dad had a small car dealership and he often drove different cars home. He had been driving a little Mini pickup for a couple of weeks and he always left the keys in the ignition. I had started up the Mini on numerous occasions, backed it out of the garage, and maneuvered it around the driveway. I was prepared to wash my father's vehicles from top to toe just for the thrill of starting the engine and driving them around in the driveway. I would practice parking and reverse maneuvers. I was nearly fifteen years old with another whole year to wait before my father would let me get my license. I had already spent hours with my father's assistance preparing an old

1952 Citroën, my first car, which sat gleaming in the carport waiting to be driven. The wait was agony. I was a natural behind the wheel and loved the idea of freedom on the open road.

I looked at the little white Mini sitting on the concrete garage floor and thought, 'Why not? How hard could it be?' Because it was a Mini, which I was familiar with, I felt more confident. Once I was on the main road, it was pretty well a straight run to Pamela's door. My friend was sick and she needed me.

It was just the sort of impulsive behavior you would expect of a fourteen-year-old. The evening sun was shining and I had no thought about having to drive home in the dark, driving on a main highway for the very first time for more than twenty miles, or checking the weather report, not to mention huge trucks thundering down the highway at 50 mph. There was not a thought of being caught by a traffic officer or by my parents. I would just make sure I stuck to the speed limit and put the Mini back in the garage. No one would be any the wiser and after all . . . my friend needed me.

My mind was made up. I set off fearlessly on my adventure. I check the fuel gauge and there is plenty of petrol. Everything is new to me and driving requires my complete concentration. I find that as long as my mind and heart are focused on my friend's need, I feel an inner calmness devoid of fear. I remember looking at the enormous wheels of a truck, as tall as my driver's window, as its brakes squealed to a halt at the traffic lights.

'I should be terrified,' I thought, but I was not. There was no doubt in my mind that I would reach my friend in complete safety. With my heart leading the way, I experienced nothing but *courage*.

I tried to accelerate up to the speed limit on the open road, but being in a little car so close to the road I felt like I was truly zooming along. My hands clutched the steering wheel. At no point was I concerned for my welfare, but every nerve in my body was alert. Various cars passed me at what seemed breakneck speed, and at one time the grill of a large truck loomed in my rearview mirror. I was relieved when he had to turn off to the timber mill.

Pamela's driveway had a tricky access, which meant crossing to the other side of the road near a corner. I had been studying the road code in preparation for getting my license. I indicated and pulled well off to the left of the highway opposite Pamela's driveway to let the traffic pass. I built up the courage when the road was clear to cross the two lanes. This was not a good time to stall.

Safely outside Pamela's house, she squealed with excitement to see me. The sun was setting and I made myself busy cutting kindling for the fire and carrying in some logs. It was midwinter and very chilly. I soon had a roaring fire in the hearth and found soup that Pamela's mum had left in the fridge to heat on the stove. We lit candles and incense and Pamela looked like a Cheshire cat that could not get the grin off her face as she sat cross-legged cuddled into the oversized armchair with blankets, hot water bottle, and a hot, steaming mug of soup.

We had been talking and laughing for a couple of hours over numerous cups of tea, soft drinks, and potato crisps when the room lit up with a brilliant flash of lightning. We waited for the rolling thunder that followed. Suddenly, the heavens opened, and it was like a fire hose was directed onto the windows as rivers of water washed over the house.

I still felt the odd shiver as my body continued to warm under my duvet. It was late when I heard my parents come in. Dad popped his head into my bedroom as I lay facing the wall and then he headed off downstairs to bed.

I held my breath as I heard the familiar sounds of my father leaving early for work. To my amazement the wee Mini fired up and he drove off up the driveway.

Home free! All was okay in my world as I skipped off to school. I told no one about my ordeal, not even my sisters, and I swore Pamela to silence. I could not risk it ever getting back to my parents.

After the good thirty-minute walk it took to get home from school, I opened the front door, my normal cheerful self, only to see my mother's face deadly serious. My heart sank. How could she possibly know?

"Your father has never been so angry with you. He will deal with you when he gets home."

That was all she said, and in some ways that was tougher than the whack I was preparing myself for as I waited the two hours for my father to come home. He was an old-school disciplinarian who believed in corporal punishment as his duty as a father. He only lashed out in anger on the very rare occasion, but rather dished out punishment like something that had to be done so that we would learn our lesson. The burning welt on our bottoms with his handprint could be felt for a number of days. The trouble with that sort of discipline is that there is a fine line between love and fear.

In the most part I managed to avoid "the hidings" as we called them. It was easier to just do as you were told than to tolerate the trouble my strong-willed older sister managed to get herself into.

I heard my father's footsteps coming up the hall and he entered my room. His face looked genuinely pained. He never had to punish me and I could tell he really did not want to.

"I just can't believe you did that," he said incredulously. "Why? You must have had a good reason."

"My friend was sick. She needed me," I managed to say.

"You could have been killed or killed someone else! You know I must punish you for something so serious. This is going to hurt me as much as it hurts you."

"Yes, I know. It's okay dad." I actually felt sorry for him as I pulled my pajama bottoms down and rolled onto my side.

When he left, we both had tears in our eyes. I did not join the family for dinner that night and went to sleep still wondering how they could possibly have known.

It was midmorning earlier that day, and one of dad's customers was filling his truck with diesel.

"I towed one of your girls home in that storm last night," he chatted matter of factly.

"Nuh, can't have been my girls," dad replied. "None of them have got their driver's license."

"Yep, that's the Mini over there," he pointed to the car. "Damn things are so low to the ground I suppose it got water in the carburetor. It was fair hosing down. I dropped her at the top of your drive in Whau Valley."

A farmer who lived in the middle of nowhere who just happened to be a customer at our service station who just happened to know my father's address. What were the chances of that, eh?

I discovered important things about myself that night. I had a compassionate heart that spoke louder than my fears when another was in need.

I had complete faith in my own abilities even if my actions appeared foolish.

Even though I knew right from wrong and was not predisposed to breaking the law, I was capable of overriding rules and regulations that the majority felt they must follow. I was capable of engaging a strong willpower when I believed that what I must achieve was more important than playing by the rules.

I weighed up the risk of the consequences versus what I believed to be right action and confronted risk head-on without fear.

The most significant insight I received was that when the heart was engaged and when action was inspired by an open heart, there resided *courage*. I could be right on the edge of my comfort zone, but an open heart allowed my energy to fully flow through my body, bringing peace where *courage* and all manifestation is born.

Once I allowed myself to experience fear and doubt during the storm, I was in a state of anxiety, which was depleting my energy flow, and guess what? My worst fears were about to appear. I had doubt for my safety and was not safe. I had doubt about making it home and the car failed. I feared that my parents would discover the truth and they did.

The God force in me, which is totally abundant in its ability to manifest anything, will obey all thoughts, both positive and negative. The laws of manifestation do not discern what is a good thought and what is bad, that which will deliver a good outcome and that which will not. We are the disciplinarians of our thoughts and thus the masters of our reality.

When I engaged my heart, which was the driving force behind my action, I experienced courage that allowed the potentially fearful experience of driving to my friend to be an effortless and successful event. Once I experienced fear and doubt, the outcome of events quickly deteriorated.

Apply this to any potentially fearful life experience.

Let us say that I invest in real estate and borrow a few million dollars. Can the investments service the debt? Have I calculated in the possible loss of rents, repairs and maintenance, price increases to rates, insurance, or mortgage rates?

The majority opinion may be, "It is not a good time to invest in real estate. You need a 9 percent net return to cover all possibilities and be safe and currently you will only achieve 5 percent."

Up comes fear. "I'm out here rowing my own waka. No one else appears to be taking the risk."

I could take on the doubts of others and succumb to fear that will immobilize me or I can calmly trust my own calculations and continue with *courage*. With a small cash injection, I can increase the size of the investment and my net income figures come in at a 10 percent return. Alternatively, I can redecorate for a little extra cost and fit the stylish kitchen I have stored in my garage. In a private sale the house sells for $30,000 more than I paid for it, a $25,000 net profit in six weeks. I make a calculated decision and get on with it in present time and discipline my mind not to wander into thoughts of the possibility of what might happen.

There is only so much I can calculate and then there is a time when positive action is required, having faith in my ability to manifest with no written guarantees. Fears must be confronted and quieted. If fear belongs in *future time* of "what if?" then I must trust my calculations, make my investment decision, and get on with that decision in *present time* without prolonged worry about the future. If my mind remains undisciplined with fearful thoughts, I am no longer "earthing" my energy in present time via the base chakra and manifestation becomes blocked and distorted.

Courage to succeed begins with the discipline of thought, which insists I stop the wandering of the mind into future possibility and stay in the moment with the task at hand. Only in the calmness of the moment can the heart stay open, which allows the energy to flow fully into the lower body. This is necessary for the ease of manifestation into physical reality.

You will have heard people say, "It's just not flowing" or "I gave it a go and it went well for a while but fizzled out" or "yeah, it was okay for a while, but I got tired of it."

What about emotional *courage?*

Our fears in relationships can be numerous:

- "She won't be attracted to me as I grow older."

- "Men are incapable of being faithful."

- "He turned out just like I thought he would."

- "I knew he would stray about the time of the 'seven year itch.'"

- "I was always worried she would have her mother's need to control."

- "My relationships never last more than three years."

- Or a classic someone said to me once, "You might love me now, but wait until you really know me."

Talk about setting yourself up to fail. This is from someone who cannot possibly like themselves and has no faith in themselves. It is not hard to work out what those inner thoughts are likely to manifest.

We will manifest our fears just as we will manifest our positive intentions. When we really trust the great beings that we are, we learn to follow our own intuition, our own knowingness.

"On this day, I open my heart and see all that is good in my partner. I recognize the divine spirit that she is, and as I see the essence of her perfection. That perfection is also me."

As you hold that thought, you experience the opening of your heart and the awakening of the knowingness of who you really are. Your mind is not wandering into your fears of the future or your resentments of the past. Then you are only left with the decision of what is it that you want.

When you know what it is you want, the doing is effortless.

Do your calculations. Make your decisions with the enthusiasm of an open heart and go forth with *Courage*.

Night Lights: 15 Years Old

Teaching: Intuition

My forehead feels numb. My sinuses are like deep, icy rivers as I pull my woolen scarf over my nose and cheeks. The drone of my friend John's 650cc motorcycle reverberates incessantly in my helmet and I am relieved we are on the last stretch of road home. It is winter and our fun day has closed suddenly into night. At fifteen years old, I am expected to be home before nightfall. My parents will not be too pleased. I feel the familiar grimy feeling and the taste of car exhausts after a long journey. My buttocks are sore and my legs are more than ready to stretch. Not long now, as we roar down the Ruakaka straights into Whangarei.

I watch the lights. A pretty row of orange balls away off in the distance not unlike the lights that welcome you into a small town. The double trailer stock truck in front of us has exhaust problems and its fumes threaten to asphyxiate us. John takes the opportunity to pass on the long familiar stretch of road he has traveled so many times in the past. He pulls out into the opposite lane. The bike lurches forward. This is what I love the most.

The deep throb of the motor vibrating with the surge of acceleration pushing me hard against the backrest. Raw power. Free.

Every hair on the back of my neck stands to scream alert. A pulse rages down my spine, throwing my hips and thighs into violent contraction against John's lightweight frame. The sudden jolt of my body is like a red alert to John. He does not know if I am having an epileptic fit or falling from the bike, so in a split-second decision he abandons the lengthy passing of the truck and slips back in behind the tailgate. He has every intention of pulling to the side of the road as soon as possible to see if I am all right.

I can still see the shine of the chrome grill and feel the sudden whoosh of warm air against my face as a truck with its top row of orange cab lights thunders past us through the night. It has no headlights. I feel the shudder of the bike and my nylon jacket is sucked against my body with the force of the wind draft. There is a moment of recollection that we have been inches away from certain death and then I am gone, out of there . . . somewhere.

I have no memory of John pulling well off the road or getting off the bike. My first memory is that he needs my help as he struggles to remove his helmet. His hands are shaking so violently he cannot release the catch. He wants to be sick as he steadies himself with one hand grasping at the handlebars, bent over, retching. His shoulders and arms are in full contraction now, shaking and trembling. He cannot stop repeating, "You saved my life! My God . . . you just saved my life!"

I reach for him and pull him hard towards me, instinctively squeezing him tight.

I knew in that moment that it was not my time to leave this Earthly dimension.

We stand like this for what seemed a very long time, shivering in the still night with the stars ablaze. Alive.

I have little recollection of getting home that night or ever talking to anyone about it, not even John. It was as if we could not bring ourselves to revisit the harsh reality that we had just had a near-death experience. I mumbled apologies to my father and went to bed. I left for Auckland city the next year with lazy days and motorbikes a thing of the past. John went on to drive within the safety of his father's solid old Mark 2 Zephyr.

I did not think about that night for many years. What stayed with me always, however, was the knowledge that we were more than these physical bodies and more than our five senses. My body carried a divine intelligence. It knew things. My earlier dabbling in Christian teachings would have told me it was a watchful angel or guide at work, or Jesus himself. It was possibly all of the above and I knew that it was inside my body. The energy of all the angels, all the spirit guides, and all the great spiritual teachers was the same energy that lived in me.

To see, hear, taste, touch, and smell. The five senses we rely upon every day in this dimension. They are part of how we define ourselves.

People talked about a woman's intuition, a vague remnant from a time long gone. Why women? For the same reason nearly all the witches that were burned for over 400 years were women. Women kept the feminine energy alive where all other sensory perception resided. They and a few male wizards and warlocks developed more than their five senses. They possessed the wisdom of knowingness or intuition and spoke telepathically through thought. They understood that the frequencies of color and sound directly affected the field of energy that surrounded the body and also the animals and plants; in fact, all that was physical. They practiced the healing arts and understood the healing power of plants for their medicinal properties. Even to dabble in any of the above, one was considered to be practicing witchcraft.

You can hear the powers that be, "Witchcraft must be stamped out!"

You cannot have the general populous running around knowing that they are channels for the all-powerful God force that is pure love, pure joy, and all-knowing. That does not sound like something that can be controlled, molded, or contained in a society that must play by the rules.

If people are limited to only five senses and indoctrinated by fear, they can be placed en masse into servitude. They can be given strict rules to live by and accept the punishment handed down should they question it. That left a very few in charge with an army of ants standing to attention. Now that is looking easier to monitor.

"We need a few million in the factories and mines from sunrise to sunset so there is money in the government vaults. Don't worry, they won't question not having a life of their own for they know no different and nor did their parents."

Every face as far as the eye can see is in the same boat. What have they to think about except the gnawing hunger in their bellies and the brief relief of payday?

"Let us have another few million in the corporate offices. Because they earn more than everyone else and accumulate lots of 'stuff,' they will believe they are free. They will not be. They will be tied to a clock, a dress code, a speech code, a 'be seen there' code, and a spend code. By the time they cover the costs of their private schools, their university educations, their exorbitant mortgages to enable them to reside on the right side of town, and all that 'stuff' they have been programmed to desire, they will be as trapped and as controlled as the factory worker."

The whole lot of them will have long forgotten that they are great beings that can manifest anything, that they are the most evolved species on the planet with dominion over all others, that they can change everything in their material world by changing their minds.

"Don't worry, they won't give us any trouble. They are too tired, too undernourished, and too downtrodden by the monotony of their lives to bother trying."

Religion and politics are firmly in bed together.

"If the government departments of bureaucracy and the Armed Forces can't keep you in line, we will rely upon your own guilt for disappointing God. Nothing like guilt to keep you on the straight and narrow."

The one thing they make sure of is that you cannot know that you are free to live as you please, and that you create every next moment in your world through the power of your thoughts, your emotions, and your spoken word. As long as you are suppressed under the veil of ignorance, you will continue to desire pleasure from an exterior source rather than the bliss and inspired creativity of your great God force. All those *things* you desire should keep you sufficiently indebted to corporate banks and money lenders, which will stoke the bellows of your fear—the driving force that gets you up in the morning, and to shower, dress, eat, and join all the other ants on motorways, buses, and trains all over the world to be somewhere all day or night that you don't really want to be.

You moan when it is Monday or the end of your holidays, patiently waiting for the joy of Friday because for a moment you will be free. Free to drown your sorrows in alcohol or finally have time to care for yourself and your family. This brief window of *freedom* is quickly filled with tasks like shopping, laundry, house cleaning, children's sports, or elderly parents, and then it all starts again; working to live to pay for stuff that you are barely home to enjoy. The stress and disharmony builds and all you know is that you are not truly happy. You might change your job, your home, or your spouse, or move to another country. This will satisfy your need for excitement and new creativity for a while, but without the peace of your inner spiritual journey all of it is temporary, empty, and shallow.

If we sat residing on a planet of higher frequency observing Earth, we would be dumbfounded at the futility of the residents' efforts to find true happiness. No wonder the more sensitive children arriving on Earth become completely disillusioned by the time they are teenagers. They do not want the robotic existence of their parents. Their parents are not happy, so what is the purpose of existence? Everywhere they look, the planet is in a mess due to the greed of the few versus the suffering of the masses. If they are born into poverty, they do not want to accept the limited lives of their parents working endlessly—for what? So that they are warm enough and dry enough at night and can afford to feed themselves so that they can go back to work? The young people are asking the important questions and are rising up en masse to challenge political decisions that assist the wealthy and keep the others firmly in their place oiling the cogs of *progress*. When did we forget that the power resides within each of us? We have always been great creative beings worthy of joy and ease. En masse we are an unstoppable force. The mountain of change will not move by raging discontent and protesting, yet good on the front line for airing the issues! It is only through the power of our ability to love that our I AM presence can flow through us to instantly manifest change. We must discipline our emotions of fear, anger, and grief if we are to tap into this uncontainable, infinite power within us.

I remembered how every hair on the back of my neck stood up and the involuntary jerks that wracked by body when I was in life-threatening danger. The knowledge of the intelligence that came from within me unprompted by any exterior source awakened something in me with a flood of consciousness and spiritual sensitivity.

I became an observer of the world, working consciously to live with joy and freedom with a stoic refusal to be trapped into any activity that I did not want to participate in.

Some within the ant farm of government departments tried to stop me at one point, to put me in my place.

"How can you live like that, when I have to live like this? You must have attained wealth through criminal activities and it is your job to *prove* that you did not!"

It took ten years before they apologized profusely and offered me compensation.

There were others along the journey that were inflamed with jealousy, sadly not understanding that this emotion would extinguish their inner power more efficiently than any other, making all that they desired vaporize before them.

I am no longer limited to my five senses. I can feel energy, see colors and pictures with my eyes closed, hear guidance, send telepathic messages that can be received and intuitively know things like when a friend is about to call. *In* this world, but no longer *of* this world.

⇐ 5 ⇒

Night Nurse: 17 Years Old

Teaching: Guidance

The old building creaked and groaned and the nearby trees cast eerie shadows on the walls like wandering spirits from times past. I shuddered as I glanced over my shoulder to see movement within the gloom and semi-expected a hand to clamp down on my shoulder. There were stories about how the building was used for the criminally insane until a locked facility out of town became preferable. Some nights the wind would howl and I swore I could hear the screams of demented minds and the results of torturous shock therapy. There was an old room out the back with a chipped concrete floor and a central drain. It was now used for storing equipment. Old Mr. Biggs, who had been an orderly at the hospital forever, told me one night in a hushed tone, "This is where they lined them all up to remove all the feces and vomit. They just hosed them down en masse. Not even any hot water in them days."

I remember the shock and horror I felt as I imagined the naked bodies huddled together and screaming. It felt like I had been punched in the stomach and winded. Times like that, I questioned if I was ever of this world with all of its atrocities. I felt sure that wherever I had come from, no such things happened and I felt consistently shocked by the anger and abuse bereft of any sense of love that people were capable of.

I would find myself talking to the lost souls as I wandered the dimly lit corridors, "Be at peace. Be at peace. May the angels in heaven be with you and uplift you."

The Eye Ward was situated in the most ancient part of Auckland Hospital.

It was 4 a.m. on the night shift; always the hardest time to stay awake as my biorhythms were turned upside down and everything in my being screamed sleep!

With my small flashlight in hand, it was time to do the rounds. Mr. Jacobson was on hourly observations whereby he required the light of the flashlight shone into each eye to see how well the pupils were responding. Mrs. Gallaher needed antibiotics put through her intravenous line, which Staff Nurse Sally O'Brien would do as she did her drug round. There were temperatures to check and a couple of blood pressures to take.

I shivered as a branch scratched the glass window. It was like a fingernail down a blackboard, which set up a tingling up and down my spine. My eyes darted left and right as a shadow moved past a door and a dim light danced over the far wall.

"Be at peace. May the angels in heaven be with you and uplift you."

"What is that you are saying, dear? I can't hear you and I can't see you."

Dear Miss Perkins was in her eighties and sat propped up in bed wide awake with bandages over both eyes. She had had her cataracts removed. The story went that her only son returned from England to find that his mother was completely blind and had been so for three years without visiting her doctor. The removal of the advanced cataracts would restore her sight.

"Hello, Miss Perkins. What are you doing wide awake?" I playfully scolded.

"Call me Ivy, dear. I haven't been called Miss Perkins since I taught my primary school class," she chuckled. "I have always liked this time of day. The 'work-a-day world' is still and I feel closer to God."

I just wanted to squeeze her, she was so gorgeous. Her cheeks were smooth and unlined and her hair was a natural brilliant white without any sign of yellowing. Her hands were clasped across her upper tummy and there were clear signs of arthritis in her nobbled knuckles and large protruding veins where the skin was thin.

"I am so excited nurse. I get my bandages off this morning and my doctor says I will see again! I still can't quite believe it," she giggled like an excited schoolgirl.

"How marvelous!" I exclaimed. "The next time I see you, you will see me!"

"Yes, yes! I can't wait. I just know that you are pretty. I can hear it in your voice."

"What? You can hear prettiness?" I said, teasing her.

"Yes, there is a deep kindness in your voice and that is always beautiful," she said with a grin exposing ancient archaic dental work that shone silver and gold in the dim light.

"You're something else, Ivy."

"Something other than myself, dear? No, I don't think so," she laughed.

It was hard to know if Ivy was playing with me or not. All I knew was that we were kindred spirits and she was easy to love. In that moment in the low glow of her bedside light, we were a million miles away from the horrors the hospital walls could speak of. She was a wonderful mixture of wisdom and optimism. In the short time she had known me, she seemed to see me with greater clarity than most others, even from within her world of darkness.

I so wanted to see her delight after her many years surrounded in shadow and her last three years encased in a thick velvet blackness. I felt regret that I would leave the ward at 7 a.m. It then dawned on me that, as a student, I needed six dressings signed off as "adequately completed" before I moved on to my time on the medical ward.

"Just give me a minute, Ivy. I will be back soon."

I scooted to the office and asked Staff Nurse O'Brien if she would witness a dressing procedure for me as the patient was scheduled for today and was already awake.

"No, leave it for the morning staff. They will do it before the doctor's rounds." She took another mouthful of biscuit and sipped her tea while working on the newspaper crossword puzzle.

"Please, can I do it Staff Nurse? Ivy has not been able to see for three years and she can't wait. It is so exciting!"

Staff Nurse O'Brien looked up over her glasses and scowled at my enthusiasm.

"We don't do dressings in the middle of the night . . . and . . ."

She stopped mid-sentence as she saw the disappointment on my face.

"Very well," she sighed. "Get your trolley and disinfect it."

She rose from the comfort of her armchair and stretched.

"My morning does not start this early," she muttered and secretly smiled when she heard me humming as I collected my dressing pack and prepared my trolley.

"The eagerness of youth," she smiled with a tinge of sadness. She remembered feeling like that when she was a young bubbly student full of hope and expectation.

I carefully unwound the crepe bandage that wound around Ivy's head until the two thick cotton eye pads were exposed. I removed the first stained pad to expose Ivy's soft crinkled eyelid and carefully wiped the eye, removing a soft crust from her lashes. Her eye slowly opened and her smile broadened.

"Glory, glory, glory," she whispered. "I told you, you were pretty," and she managed a wink.

"You can see!?" I asked.

"Yes, dear . . . I can see." Ivy's voice was reverent with a deep gratitude.

The second eye was soon cleaned and Ivy let her first tears roll down her face.

"Hey, stop that!" I chided her. "You will be seeing all blurry again."

Staff Nurse O'Brien wiped her eyes and sniffed. As I turned to look at her, she quickly turned away.

"Well, done nurse. Yes, job well done." She turned on her heel and returned to the nurse's station.

Ivy beamed from ear to ear as I packed up the dressing trolley.

"Is there anything else I can get you, Ivy? Would you like to go for a walk?"

"Oh yes, dear, I would like that very much. Glory be when the sun rises!" she enthused. "There is one thing I very much would love. . . " Her voice trailed off as if wistfully thinking about the past.

"What is that Ivy?"

I moved to stand right beside her.

"I used to read palms and have been unable to see the fine lines for a very long time. Could I read yours?" she asked tentatively.

"Of course you can. I would be honored."

I pulled up a chair and moved the bedside light to allow direct light on my palm.

Ivy held my hand in hers. Her palms were dry and callused from a lifetime of hard work.

"Thank you, dear," she said looking into my eyes.

"I knew your eyes would be blue." I smiled.

Ivy found an old pair of glasses in her top drawer and then with great concentration she ran her fingertip over my palm. She took her time with the odd audible sound.

"Hmmm," she purred. "Ah ha . . . hmmmm."

"What Ivy? What is hmmm?" I said expectantly.

"Lovely clear lines. Strong direction and very little clutter from your past. Hmmm . . . You will find your partner much later in life," she finally spoke.

"Oh, I suppose I will be forty!" I stated with exasperation.

Forty seemed *so* old and so far away.

"Yes, you will be all of that dear," Ivy nodded wisely.

My heart sank. I have to wait forever to find my love.

"You will travel extensively together," she continued.

"Oohh . . . look at this!" she exclaimed excitedly. "You will be responsible for the wise distribution of a very large amount of money."

I was surprised. I was a student nurse earning $95 a fortnight, living in the nursing home, having just left home with $200 in my ASB savings account. What she said sounded like a foreign language and was nothing that had ever entered my consciousness, nor was it likely to. Well it was there now.

"Is there anything else?" I asked inquisitively.

"No dear, that is all," she yawned. "I want to read the magazine my son bought me. Me reading! Who would have thought! Thank you and bless you dear."

"Thank you, Ivy." I kissed her gently on the cheek. Her skin felt soft like tissue paper against my lips. "I will check on you before I leave."

Guidance comes from what is often referred to as our guardian angel. This is, in fact, our Christ consciousness, which is like a spiritual mirror of our physical form vibrating at a much higher frequency. It sits between our physical body and our I AM presence, that which we have always been and what we seek to reunite with as our bodies return to a higher frequency through our ability to love. Our "higher consciousness" for want of a better term, is the "all knowing" essence of ourselves that the majority of us are no longer conscious of because of our insistence on focusing on Earth-bound physical matter and emotions rather than the true nature of our God selves. This knowing self will give us a message or sign as many as three times, at which point, if we still do not heed the message, the communication will cease and the higher self will attempt communication with our more-dense "body self" at a later date when we are perhaps more accessible in a dream state or a meditative state.

It is the higher-frequency God force within the old woman that she taps into which is all knowing that allows her to bring forth accurate guidance for me. Everything the old woman said has come and is coming to pass. This has helped to cement the truth for me, that there is an all-knowing force within us that we can learn to access. It is just a matter of how will you tap into it and what quantity and quality will you let yourself have.

When people rely on *guidance*, they are tuning in to the voice within. If God's presence, or spark, is within each of us, then all knowingness and all love is also us. We are no longer putting God as an entity outside ourselves, but as a full working partner within us.

The flame of God Perfection lives within the human heart. There are three flames: blue (energy and power), gold (wisdom and illumination), and pink (divine love). These combined make up the Violet Flame of our perfected I AM presence. The original plan when entering physical form was to draw from universal light substances any form you desired through the power of the flame. You could design and materialize food, clothing, shelter, temples, or anything you desired or required. Your feelings energized the thoughtforms and manifestation occurred instantly. When mankind no longer rested his attention on the God presence, but more on human creation, the flame became severely reduced in size. The voice of guidance became quiet and the heart became cluttered with worldly hurts until the flame could barely be seen. Manifestation became a struggle and so the vicious circle continued as more of our focus became consumed with worldly matters. It is our imbalance away from the sacred, the pure, and all that is honest that dampens our flame until we risk once again, struggling in the dark.

Ivy teaches me that I can learn to hear a voice within me that speaks the truth. It is the word of God. The clearer I become in my ability to be peaceful without emotional reaction, becoming more the observer, the more the God-Force and its divine wisdom can come through me. There is an unlimited supply. The energy that is God and that which is the divine I AM presence are one and the same and cannot be separated.

It is time to stop seeking the answers outside of ourselves and to focus on the guidance within. Guidance is always there and will plant many seeds that germinate should we heed the messages.

For many years after my experience with Ivy, I believed that you had to seek spiritual attainment to eventually become the light of Christ consciousness. There were examples throughout the East of chelas (students) practicing endless disciplines on their quest to attain enlightenment. I remember reading the story of a man who was still holding his arm up above his head after thirty-five years as proof to his guru (teacher) how committed he was to his path of righteousness and the extent of his great discipline. He clearly had a strong belief that to become enlightened he must endure the commitment of extreme physical discipline. This was the path he followed. It was not right or wrong. It was his choice. In the same way, I could choose the discipline of loving thoughts and actions without judgment, which would steadily raise my consciousness. Sometimes I would succeed wonderfully and sometimes I would again be drawn into the density of human mind and emotions as I failed miserably.

Earth is a planet of free will, and what we focus our thoughts on becomes our reality. When I insisted on feeling anger, hurt, and judgment for others, I ultimately only hurt myself as I closed off my heart in those moments and separated myself further from the divinity of my true self.

The more I yearned for higher consciousness through study, the more it would evade me until I was willing to live in the purity that I had always been. This was the discipline.

This would require a choice to endeavor to have only loving thoughts and actions, to avoid foods and beverages that made my body dense and sluggish, and to master overindulgence in all physical pleasures; not as a hardship, but as a state of joy and clarity.

That night on the Eye Ward, I learned from Ivy Perkins that when we are in a state of love, enthusiasm, and genuine giving, we are closer to our Christ consciousness, which can then communicate with us as guidance. I received insights into my future that my true self already knew and I was simply able to hear them. In the all-knowingness of higher consciousness, there was no such thing as time, past or future; it simply was. What appeared to be an old woman able to tell my future was a woman capable of great love that was able to clear the clutter of denser frequency, enabling her to be in her all-knowing or higher self. She had steadily attained this ability throughout her life through her decision to live a charitable life with honesty and integrity whereby she extended her ability to love through compassion for others. This process would have accelerated in the years of complete darkness when there was less sensory input from the distraction of sight (i.e., she was *IN* this world but became less *OF* this world as she spent more time alone within). Regular time in a meditative state can replicate this.

Ivy reading my palm was more for my benefit than hers. The same as the old folk reading tea leaves, the soothsayers reading a crystal ball, laying the tarot cards, or throwing the runes. These were all vehicles or ritual to help trigger what they already knew.

An interesting phenomenon happens when you are hearing the truth. It resonates deep inside you and you hold the memory of what is said. I have remembered exactly what Ivy said for thirty-seven years as if it were yesterday.

There is divine *guidance* within every one of us. When we live in the peace of an open heart, we are able to access it.

≈ 6 ≈

Hawai'i: 18 Years Old

Teaching: Money

I stretched out on the double bed with its pink faded bedspread and looked around the room with a smile on my face. There was a tiny kitchen, a yellow tiled bathroom, two comfortable chairs, and a three-legged coffee table that showed the cup rings of many hot drinks. It was the Ritz as far as I was concerned, and mine for one month of blissful holiday.

I had boldly written to every hotel within two blocks of Waikiki Beach on the island of Oahu in the Hawai'ian Islands, asking them for their monthly room rate. My wee room had nothing fancy like air conditioning, but I was completely comfortable under a sheet with a three-speed ceiling fan. The wire mesh over the windows was the true Godsend as the mosquitos were the size of baby crickets.

The weekly tariff on my modest accommodation was the same as one night in the neighboring high-rise hotel with an ocean view. It took three minutes to walk through to the white sands of Waikiki Beach. I was pretty chuffed that on my student nurse wages I had managed to manifest this overseas adventure.

On my first day, I ventured down to the beach for a swim before the heat of the midday sun. After drying myself off, I stopped to watch a Hawai'ian man making flax hats. His fingers moved like quicksilver, and in no time he had produced a sturdy hat with a wide brim. I had to have one.

Onie introduced himself and set about measuring the circumference of my head with one strand of flax.

"You have a large head," he commented. "Hmm . . . open mind."

Onie was a slight man, short in stature with long wispy hair and beard, probably in his late fifties. To me, at eighteen years old, I considered him to be old with a wise, chiseled, deeply sun-tanned face. I noted his flexibility as he sat fully cross-legged and could rise unaided and effortlessly to a standing position. We chatted while he worked the flax skillfully.

As I paid him and thanked him for the lovely hat, he spoke in a soft, gracious tone. "Can I take you for breakfast tomorrow?"

I had the fleeting thought, 'Surely an old fellow like this is not hitting on me.'

There was something so very gentle about Onie that I instinctively trusted him.

"Yes, okay. That would be nice," I said, returning his smile and a little bemused.

I did not know anyone on the island and being with someone local was appealing. I felt safe with Onie because he was so much older than me. More like a grandfather.

I let him know where I was staying and right at 9 a.m. there was a light "rata tat tat" on my door. He took me to a nearby hotel for a delicious breakfast of island fruits, bacon and eggs, and great coffee. I remember thinking, 'He can't make that much money making hats' as I offered to pay my share.

He would not hear of it.

"It was my invitation to you," he smiled.

He walked me back to my hotel room and simply said, "See you, same time tomorrow."

Before I had time to answer or dispute this, he had turned and gone. This same routine happened for the next three mornings. Not once did he try to touch me or flirt with me inappropriately. It seemed to be a genuine platonic friendship. I finally said to him, "Onie, I am not comfortable with you spending all your money on me."

"Money? That is not a problem. It is merely the exchange of energy. Is there something else you would like to do?"

"Well," I said thoughtfully, "I would like to see around the island sometime."

"Good!" he seemed pleased. "Shall we go now?"

"Great. Is there a bus we can catch?" I replied enthusiastically.

"Walk with me," Onie quietly replied.

My first thought was that this agile, slender man wanted to walk around the island!

He was a man of few words. I did not question where we were going and decided to just go with the flow. This was the first time we had walked the main streets together and I noticed that whenever we passed a local Hawai'ian they would nod acknowledgement to Onie. I soon realized that he knew a great deal of people and locals held him in high esteem.

We turned a corner and walked into a car rental company.

"Choose the car for us to travel in," he said matter of factly.

There were Cadillacs, Continentals, Buicks, Desotos, Fords, Chevrolets, topless Jeeps, and there at the back was the most gorgeous bright red convertible Mustang.

"What?" I looked at him in disbelief. "Anything . . . any one that I want?"

"Whatever you want," he stated.

A tall Hawai'ian gentleman came out of the office with a broad smile and clasped Onie's hand in both of his, overtly expressing his delight in seeing him.

"He knows the owner," I observed.

"The red Mustang," I called to Onie without hesitation.

Onie waved with thumbs up and returned from the office with the key in hand.

That was us. The warm trade winds in our hair cruising down the highway on our great adventure to Sunset Beach. I could not wait to see the huge surf that I had read about. I felt as if I had died and gone to heaven. I laughed out loud as I watched the long greying strands of Onie's hair blowing gently around his face and felt intense gratitude for the generosity of my unlikely friend.

I had the most magnificent day as Onie showed me the sights and we met up with surfers smoking joints on the beach.

"Acapulco Gold," they informed me. "The best in the world."

I sat for what seemed a long time after that blissed out in the North Shore sun.

The stories of the shallow reefs and the possibility of instant death if you fell off your board horrified me as I watched the surfing gladiators on their steep descent down mountainous waves.

Onie dropped me outside my little hotel at dusk.

"I have to leave the island in the morning, but I will be back by evening. Dinner?" he inquired.

"That sounds lovely," I called cheerfully as I waved goodbye.

I realized by now that Onie was clearly a man of means and he certainly did not derive his only income from making hats. Perhaps it was just something he liked to do. A way of meeting people maybe?

The following night Onie knocked on my door at about 7:30 p.m. and we walked a few blocks to yet another hotel lobby. We took the lift to the top floor where Onie had reserved a table in the window of the revolving restaurant. We had the last of the ocean views as day turned to night and the city lights began to sparkle. A large rack of lamb was brought to the table with assorted vegetables, salad, and fine champagne. At the end of a delicious meal, we had hardly made a dent in the lamb and the table was cleared.

"What happens to the rest of the lamb?" I inquired.

"Oh, it will be thrown out," said Onie casually.

I felt acute discomfort in this knowledge. I had been raised not to waste food and was only one generation away from the use of food stamps and bread buttered with animal dripping after the war. I talked about how there were hundreds of people hungry and starving in the world and that was a shocking waste of food.

"Yes," Onie agreed. "However, we paid for it, so it is ours to discard."

With the eagerness and political passion of my eighteen-year-old mind I continued, "Don't you think it would be right and proper for food and other resources to be more evenly shared, Onie?"

"Yes I do. It is called Socialism in the present systems we have."

We debated how it was not right for a system to not reward the man with initiative and hard work versus the person who was lazy and milked the system for as much as they could, but ideally there could be a system where *everybody wins*. Not possible in the world as we know it, but completely feasible in a time of higher-frequency energy.

"You are thinking of a time in the future," Onie declared. "Creating that future is why we are here."

I was left pondering his words as we departed the restaurant. The disappearing roast lamb still did not sit well with me. The joy just seemed to leave me at this time. I was aware that I had spent every day with Onie for a week. Our outings were becoming increasingly lavish and extravagant. As we sat enjoying special coffees in a local bar, I found the courage to ask him what he wanted from me.

"There is nothing I want or need from you. I enjoy your company," he said.

"I don't mean to be ungrateful Onie, but I have had enough dining out. It has been very lovely, such beautiful food and champagne and I do not wish to offend you, but I only have a short time here and I would love to meet the real Hawai'ians. Where are the real Hawai'ian people, Onie?"

"You only needed to say," he said beaming. "Let's go then!"

Onie left a roll of notes on the table and offered to help me with my summer jacket.

The music pulsated with the sound of drums and ukuleles. Hot bodies and a blur of colorful hibiscus flowers printed on shirts and dresses spun around the dance floor. There was the delicious smell of food from the feast and small children giggled and chased each other.

Onie stood on the sidelines, his eyes bright as he watched me practicing the hula with two women who laughed hysterically at my attempts.

I ran to him all smiles, "This is more like it Onie. I just love this!"

He placed his hands in a prayer position and bowed deeply before me. His sudden reverence stopped me in my tracks.

"You are a fast learner," he quietly stated.

He kissed my forehead, turned, and was gone.

It took me a while to realize that he was not coming back. I mulled over his final words as one of the older Hawai'ian women came up to me.

"Where has your friend Onie gone?"

"You know him?" I exclaimed excitedly.

"Yes, he is a visiting Kahuna from one of the other islands."

I looked puzzled.

"A medicine man or spiritual teacher," she explained. "He does not live here, but when we see him in the city, it is because he has been called to teach a student."

I felt stunned as I heard his words again in my mind.

"Yes, anything you want."

"Real Hawai'ians? You only needed to say."

"You are a fast learner."

The teaching I received from Onie would last me a lifetime. I was fascinated by the fact that someone who was more advanced or open spiritually could not only know that I was arriving from New Zealand, but place themselves where they would find me with the specific intention of taking me as a student. I had read somewhere that the teacher will always find their student, but did not know that I would have the experience.

The lessons I received about wealth were invaluable for a girl who came from a relative working-class background. I had witnessed people without money yearning for the things they could not have, believing that once procured, their lives would be happier and more complete. For Onie to saturate me in such luxury over such a short time period, it became obvious that there was something missing for me. To experience the laughter, dance, music, and sharing with a like-minded group brought a color, richness, and joy to my life that money alone could never do.

This teaching influenced my decisions when offered fame and fortune on more than one occasion and all of my work and investment decisions from that day on. My first questions were always "Is it my passion?" and "Will it make me truly happy?" If the answer to either of these was no, it was easy to walk away. The promise of potential millions could not sway me. Notoriety could not sway me. If the asset or action did not bring more joy and color into my life, it was not for me.

What I did not realize initially when practicing this was that doing only what I was passionate about, that which made me truly happy, kept me in the energy frequency of present time. I became more efficient with time management and could tackle more than one project at a time, all the while enthusiastically. Success was assured and manifestation appeared to be effortless. My asset base and personal wealth continued to grow, yet all the while I knew that it was creativity that was bringing me happiness.

"Money can't buy me love." (The Beatles)

Do people really believe this? Who doesn't secretly believe that a large lottery win would save a whole lot of their problems?

Onie taught me the very simple lesson that money is merely energy and that we can play with it, enjoy it, and be creative with it, but alone it is hollow. It has no real substance in that the pleasures it can buy are not the things that bring real lasting joy, and ultimately they are transient. As you question this, ask yourself if you have a jet ski or some other such toy in the garage. It is no longer that much fun and you are not that motivated to use it anymore. This is understandable and expected. We are here to make known the unknown. You now know what it feels like to roar around and around . . . been there, done that, over it, sell it to someone who is not over it. Do you remember how thrilled you were the day you bought it or the pleasure you derived from studying the various models and motors?

In understanding this, the things that money buys are not to be clung to or hoarded. To release physical possessions represents a healthy creative relationship with money. It also shows us that if money is a form of energy as all matter is, then matter can be reproduced over and over again. A good example of this is when you see the bankrupt get back on his or her feet, apply the same principles of success, and make another few million dollars in just a few years.

I recall a friend saying to me, "How could you sell that beautiful classic sports car?"

"Because it is a thing. A saleable item that can be replaced."

I had enjoyed the experience of a lovely car, so could easily let it go. The friend asking me still yearned for the experience. They imagined the pleasure, but had not drawn it through to physical manifestation yet, so it was hard for them to imagine releasing something they still lusted for.

I had heard people say how being rich would make them a whole lot happier than being poor, and that of course is true to an extent. I am happier in a new car that starts every morning than a very old car that is troublesome. Money can buy quality organic food, a comfortable warm home, the adventure of travel, and the freedom from having to work a job, allowing greater creativity. If you put the price of that ease at an income of say, $150,000 per annum in today's money (not including the servicing of debt) it would be true to say that you would not be any happier with $250,000 per annun or $500,000 per annum. You would own different, more grand things, but unless you were giving more of it away with an open heart, the extra income wouldn't necessarily make you any happier. We see from this that once we have enough to lift us out of poverty, unfulfilling work, and struggle, it is not the money making us happy. It is the freedom to be our great I AM presence, creative, philanthropic, or whatever inspires us. Initially what began with Onie as exciting indulgence in pleasures for myself developed into a consciousness of the needs of others and that seeing to my own desires alone began to feel dissatisfying, empty, and lacking in joy.

My experience of real joy and laughter came from much simpler things like playfulness, music, dance, and the feeling of love and sharing.

Most of the pleasure derived from money is the anticipation of accumulating the physical manifestation. This is true for all physical manifestation, whether it be another branch for your business expansion or a bigger garden. The planning and visualization of that which you wish to manifest is pleasurable and exciting. For example, planning a holiday and counting down the days could be more pleasurable than the holiday itself, or lusting after the ideal motorcar or boat filled in hours of time as opposed to it sitting forgotten for weeks on end, after the original novelty has worn off. Planning, designing, and building the ideal house could create hours and hours of excitement, yet living in it many years later did not prevent a bout of depression. This tells us that it is the creative process of manifestation that is inspiring. Why? Because it is our God force and true creative essence that is in motion, which is the life force. Awake, alive, and inspired equals happy because we are fully engaged in the moment, which allows our spiritual energy to flow.

Have you ever heard the person who always dreamed of having a swimming pool state a year later, "I would never own a pool again. Always having to test it and clean it and it was too cold most of the year to use the damn thing!"

Or the dream lifestyle block with cows and chickens. "I spent all my weekends working and you may as well just dig a hole and tip your money into it!"

The clue is in the title, "lifestyle block." It works wonderfully if you live your life there, not try to own it as a possession while you disappear to work to pay for it.

What has happened here? The dream has become the burden. That is exactly what an over indulgence in the physical reality feels like. You own twelve houses and then resent the repairs and the bills. You own a fleet of classic cars and then have to spend a fortune on the sheds to house them because you now have the responsibility of looking after them. You feel guilty for not getting your yacht out of the water onto dry dock and now the hull has an osmosis problem. You keep buying shoes and clothes you do not wear and then resent the fact that your wardrobe is just too small. It goes on and on. We keep getting this stuff because we have become addicted to the yearning, the lust, the anticipation of having it, and the fleeting excitement it brings. It is a trap.

What our desires tell us is that we are creative beings, and when we are co-creating with God we are truly in "our element," in our joy, making known the unknown.

Money is often the thing that people yearn for in their future, in all of its different physical forms. Unless it enriches your ability to love, share, or connects you more to your true self, it is only the yearning that gives the most pleasure while the actual manifestation of money and that which it can buy can be fleeting and hollow of any emotional fulfillment.

The same principle can be applied to our emotional relationships with others. If acquiring the relationship is based on physical attraction alone with no real emotional depth, you will soon tire of the same lover, which is no different from that shiny boat you once lusted for. Extra-marital affairs are often like taking that boat for a spin. Thrilling for a moment or so, or a few weekends.

The potential trap, that money will solve your unhappiness, is common knowledge to those who have manifested great wealth. The majority who have not, waste years in the emotions of desire, lust, and dissatisfaction. They will sacrifice precious moments with friends and family and risk physical exhaustion in the pursuit of money.

There are those who achieve wealth and success, yet the highs they receive from this repeated achievement are so addictive that they busily pursue more. How many times have we heard people say when they finally see the traps of their accumulated success, "I wish I had the time to re-live parts of my life. I would give more time to simple pleasures with the ones that I love." Or, "I wish I had devoted less time to worrying about money and simply been grateful for all the blessings I had."

There are some that consciously work at "getting it right" so that they have a good balance between inspirational work of their choice, financial abundance, and quality time with friends and family. Relaxing with the weekend barbecue, and a good laugh feels the same whether you earn X or XXX.

The one that always makes me smile is when the holiday season comes around and people finally have *time* to be in their luxury homes. They "up sticks," lock up the mansion, and "rough it" in a tent or old holiday bach. These are the times spent together that the family talk about over the years with the most fondness. They grow old and realize that it took them a lifetime of toil to learn it.

I am appreciative of Onie for assisting me with this lesson when I was so young. From that day on, it did not matter how many mansions with swimming pools I lived in or luxury cars I drove. I am aware that I am co-creating with the God force and I never have any trouble giving them up. They are material things that can all be replaced. In fact, the very process of letting go allows the inspiration of new creativity. For me, all investments must be fun, challenging, creative, and inspiring. I do not care if an industrial building is returning 11 percent net. I have no desire to own it. Money alone is not sufficient. It is interesting to me that I have heard many investment managers and experts say, "Investments should never be an emotional decision. Work with the facts and nuts and bolts of returns, not whether you like the décor."

I understand this way of thinking, but it does not work for me. Good financial returns on a bunch of grey buildings or soulless structures do not please my heart. I instead say to people, "Do what drives your passion and enthusiasm and that will engage the great being of light that you are, if you want to manifest miracles."

I am forever grateful that Onie chose me as his student and taught me that I could have anything I wanted, but a desire for money and worldly goods alone would never bring me lasting happiness.

I think about Onie and the Hawai'ian luau. The bright colors and sweet smells as I danced and danced. Days went by after that special night and I wondered if I would hear his friendly rap on my window shutters. I wanted to thank Onie, but knew that I would not see him again.

In my imagination I bow deeply with my hands in prayer position and honor his being.

❧ 7 ❧

And Who Are You?: 19 Years Old

Teaching: Sex

I stood perched on my stepladder sanding back the old sideboard in preparation for painting. It was there and then it was gone. Fast as that, like a white sheet flapping in the corner of my eye, then whipping behind me. I felt a tingling sensation right down my back, which I would learn to recognize later in my life as my ability to feel the presence of visiting spirits.

It was late at night and I was alone. I felt suddenly startled and a little fearful.

What *was* that!?

I had definitely seen it and I had felt something. You're kidding me? Ghosts really do look like white sheets? They really do feel kind of cold and electric?

This was my first home and she was nearly 100 years old. I had gone cap in hand to the bank with various guarantors and had managed to raise the necessary funds. I had often wondered how many people had shared these rooms. Ghosts? It kind of made perfect sense to me. I didn't however start up a new interest in "ghost busting" houses. It seemed to be a one off.

"And who are you?"

I was sitting bolt upright in my bed, my heart literally pounding in my chest. There was a man, less than thirty years old with thick dark hair and wearing a crisp white shirt, attending to his necktie. It was as if he had risen from my bed and was casually dressing for work.

I did not know this man. With a smile he looked at me and began to walk towards me. With my panic increasing, I demanded, "What do you want? What are you doing here!?"

I had no control over how fast my heart was pumping.

"You're frightened aren't you?" he said nonchalantly.

"You're damn right I am! What are you doing in my room?"

I felt the compression of the mattress as he sat on the edge of the bed and looked intently into my eyes.

"Don't be afraid. You will get used to it."

With that he was gone and I was lying heavily on my side. I could tell that my body had not moved as if waking from sleep, but I had not been asleep. The same shafts of morning sunlight flooded the room and the same little white-eye bird, was fluttering in the camellia bush outside my window.

He was definitely here, telling me not to be afraid. Was he a spirit? How had I been sitting bolt upright in bed, angry at the man's intrusion into my bedroom? The whole time I felt like my "normal" self and as we inter-acted, I believed myself to be wide awake. I was familiar with remembering vivid dreams and this was not a dream. Why did he behave with such familiarity? It was like I was between worlds, not fully back to my body after sleep. All I was certain of was that I was not asleep.

It was three years later when it happened again.

"What are you doing here? Why are you dancing in my room?"

I was in the upstairs bedroom of my third house, so I could no longer blame the spirits residing in the first old lady. I could hear the familiar sounds of my flatmate making a cup of tea downstairs as I sat up against the puffed up pillows of my bed.

Sheer terror best describes the feeling as I watched five, maybe six nymph-like creatures floating around my room. They were female, very slender with wafting fabric wrapped about them. Dream-like, floating wisps of pale pink and fuchsia. They appeared to be spinning and dancing around each other, floating up and over each other.

The fear is hard to describe and hard for me to understand why it felt impossible to control. These were hardly aggressive or threatening beings. What was happening was so removed from my familiar life that I was way outside my comfort zone and experienced the unknown as a threat to my safety.

I found myself shouting at them, "What do you want? What are you doing here? Go away! Leave me alone!"

There is no sound from my voice, but my message is transmitted through my thoughts as efficiently as if I had just spoken.

The young women instantly oblige and are gone.

I am lying on my left side, head buried heavily into my pillow. The clink of the cups and the sound of the electric jug continues downstairs. My first thought is, I have just had one of those experiences again, not quite back to my body. Between worlds. Who were those women and what did they want? Why do I feel so terrified?

I could hear the activity in my home. I was not asleep.

Is it simply that I have no point of reference for the experience I am having? The not knowing what is happening leaves me completely powerless. Perhaps that is the fear. To feel completely out of control.

Maybe we play with spirits like that every night while out of body; we just never remember once we are back.

The enormity of knowing I was more than my body suddenly dawned on me. I have another body that can sit up, talk, shout, and feel emotion that is not the body that appears to still be sleeping. The "light body" I was in and the "light bodies" visiting me were as real as the lady next door popping in for a cup of sugar. It seemed perfectly acceptable to me. I fly about in the night having experiences in my "light body" while the density of my physical body sleeps and rejuvenates.

"Bring it on," I called to my empty room as I swung my legs out of bed.

I will overcome this fear.

It was about a week later when they visited again. I had been crying into the night over some "waste of space" relationship, which I clearly considered important at the time. I fell asleep sad and in need of comfort.

They were close this time with their soft fabrics draping over my body like a lover's embrace. I was not having a bar of it. Animatedly, I sat forward in bed, waving my arms about in panic and shouting, "Get off! What do you want?"

All thought of overcoming my fear was long gone. I had no control over the terror I felt. This was not happening. There were no flying nymph angel things trying to stroke my body!

In the next instant, my body was thrust with intense force back into the pillows of my bed. It was enough for me to feel temporarily winded.

"Be still!"

The older woman's face was close to mine as she looked at me intently. Her voice had a soft, rich gentleness to it, but her message was strong and to the point. Her short grey hair and etched face gave her a severity that stopped me in my tracks.

"Be still," she repeated. "Now relax."

With her breathy command, my whole body seemed to melt into surrender. Suddenly I was lifting up off the mattress, floating. The nymph-like women surrounded me. All fear was gone and all I could feel was their intense love. It was a tangible force that radiated deep into my body. I understood that they wanted to comfort me. I could feel them. They really loved me. The more I relaxed, the closer they came, until the one floating directly under me came up and right through my body. The explosion of color and pure ecstasy made me gasp. Another came down through the top of my head and out through my base with an explosion of orange fire. My body leapt to attention as if experiencing spontaneous orgasm, but it was so much more than that. More than anything I had ever experienced in my physical body. Wave after wave of intense ecstasy. I was delirious with happiness, the laughter bursting from my body as I soared through the air and right through the body of one of the women. As our energies blended, I again felt intense pleasure exploding through my body. I knew in that moment that it was not possible to experience anything like the exaltation of this experience in the density of my physical body no matter how open or free I felt. The high-frequency energy was limitless. I never wanted it to end.

I was lying on my side having not moved. The church bells were still chiming down the road as they had been moments ago. It was Sunday morning. The very first thought I had was, 'So that is how you have sex without a body. . . .'

I remembered some years earlier stating to a big wide-open space, in the hope that somebody or something was listening when in fact it was a personal decree from my God self, "No one is to use my body as a channel while sending my spirit elsewhere." I had heard it was tough on the autoimmune system and I was not volunteering.

"I do not wish to be enlightened. I am here to enjoy the density of my flesh!"

I was no longer sure about the latter. There was nothing in the flesh that could even come close to that heavenly state I had experienced. If that was how I could feel when fully conscious or enlightened, I now yearned for it with a passion.

Every night for many months, before closing my eyes to sleep, I called on the women I fondly called the nymphets. I begged them to return, but they did not. It was like they were saying, "You learned what you needed to and you are no longer in crisis. You are strong now and we are needed elsewhere."

We are more than these physical bodies, and thank God for that! Aging, pain, restriction, and disease. As far as I can see, unless we can stop the aging process and simply ascend when it is time to move on, these physical bodies become more of a hindrance than a help. If that is all there is to our existence, if our body is all there is, I am going to disappear into a thousand movies, for I don't care to get out of bed!

Sex feels heavy and cumbersome after experiencing my light body and it leaves me with a distant memory of a higher-frequency body and a yearning to reinstate that level of sensitivity. This knowledge that we can exist within a higher frequency of energy becomes a driving force in my spiritual journey.

I feel fully alive and engaged in life when I am making known the unknown. I am a creative being that would slowly die in the face of monotonous repetition. Most of us move on to new creations once we have mastered something, for the very reason that we feel passionate and alive when engaged with our new creation. Observe a child that loves to learn. She comes home from school and cannot wait to continue the latest thing she is mastering. She does not differentiate between work, study or play. It is an all-consuming creativity that she loves to engage in.

With everything else in life, once you have become proficient at it, you move on and study something new. You do not achieve your doctorate in English and then go to a new university and decide to study English! Not so with sex. People want to keep repeating it over and over again often without a great deal of variation for 60 years! Perhaps this year we will study Tantra, or orgasm without ejaculation. If you orgasm more than once then I feel satisfied because I now know I must be a good lover. Mind you, it must happen every time or my fragile ego will be filled with self-doubt and guilt. I suppose I could just blame you after quoting my success with previous lovers so that *you* can feel self-doubt and guilt instead. Let's just keep repeating it. We'll call it "Healthy." We'll call it "Love." In fact, I will keep having sex with you even when it is the last thing I have energy for, just so that I know I am loved and that I am more attractive to you than anybody else. Your partner may misread this heightened interest as "I am needed so I must perform." Like any trained seal, it eventually yearns for the unexplored deep blue wilderness and not the repetition of the circus.

Does this repetition put sex in the same category as food—a physical need and desire servicing some deep need for physical release and satisfaction? Or is it an emotional need to feel that you are lovable or that your long-term partner still loves you? Somewhere in your mind you have convinced yourself that if your chosen partner only desires you, then you are the only one they love. This is about as nuts as saying, "If you love prawns, you cannot and will not love oysters."

You cannot put a restriction on love. You can *choose* not to share the intimacy of sex with another, either because you are deeply satisfied and you do not want to, or you want to create the security of a safe longevity for your relationship without the *fear* that occurs when that security is threatened. This does not mean that you cannot and will not love another or feel sexual attraction for another.

Sex can be used to build your self-worth or to balance the power imbalance in your relationship as your lover surrenders their need to you.

"If you *need* me, you are unlikely to leave me and I am safe."

You may feel empowered by the thrill of the chase as you conquer the one that showed resistance, but surely even this becomes tiresome and repetitive.

Advertising will encourage us to maintain a *healthy* sex life and bombard us with drugs to increase our circulation so we can still perform. Our general practitioners jump on this bandwagon stacked with personal perks if they *sell* their quota of drugs while assisting your *healthy* sex life, when in fact what draws blood supply to our loins is the excited passion of an open heart. You're literally a star if you can keep it up into your eighties and still want it. Why? What is wrong with a passionate interest in rhododendrons or vintage locomotives? A couple still copulating are enjoying *a successful loving marriage.*

"If my sex life is over, I experience fear, even panic. Who will massage my ego to show me how attractive I am and that I am a great lover? More to the point, does it mean that I am getting old?"

Ahh, there is that sneaky *fear of death* again.

The role models I have of people who do not have sex are old, disabled, or so unattractive no one wants them. My fear had just advanced into the stratosphere at the thought of that!

No one really wants to talk about their inevitable lack of enthusiasm for sex for fear of being seen to have a problem or being told that they are no longer loving. No one wants to feel the sadness that there really was a honeymoon phase in their relationship while they enthusiastically explored the unknown and that this phase is over. They fantasize about rekindling the feeling by going back to the first hotel they ever made love in, or sitting by candlelight in *their* restaurant. All the great movies depict love stories this way. The more they must accept that trying to recreate the past is futile, the more they fear for their security. Is my partner needing excitement with another? Who is texting her? Why is he home late again? Sadly, what we focus on is what we create, good or bad.

There will always be exceptions to the rule whereby someone genuinely enjoys sex every day of their life, but remember there are people who eat meat and potatoes every day, will sit for two hours in a motorway queue every day, and who really think a gold watch is great after fifty years in the same office.

Sex can be the pure expression of love and giving, which becomes a higher spiritual experience. Our body, our emotional and spiritual energy, are one and the same and can blend seamlessly. How many people experience sex in this purest form, based on unconditional giving without personal need and gratification? If unconditional giving was the focus, you would notice that sometimes she would prefer a cup of tea in bed, chocolate, and a one-hour foot massage.

Something in the spirit is slowly dying when we are no longer making known the unknown. After all, that is the reason for being physical in the first place, to be co-creative with God, the divine energy, to explore through physical matter that we are limitless energy and that we can manifest anything! The new feels exciting because we have not fully explored it yet.

Quality, loving sex will continue as long as the heart keeps expanding. If the love between two people grows deeper and richer and individually they continue to grow spiritually, they will continue the excitement of making known the unknown.

When we embrace the new, we feel totally present, engaged, and passionate about life, which fully connects our ability to experience love, and so the cycle of growth can continue.

The reason many do not move on to these greater bliss-filled creative heights is the fear of stepping outside of the familiar comfort zone that represents security. This enables people to stay in loveless abusive relationships or to endure monotonous, predictable lives, rather than risk life alone or face the unknown. When did we forget that the unknown is the essence of life itself? About the time that we forgot that we were sparks of the great I AM presence. Free, joyous beings creating our own reality, content whether we are alone or with another.

After generations of our ancestors experiencing physical and emotional hardship, putting one step in front of the other working to live rather than living to work, our lives are bereft of role models to remind us of another way. There is talk in whispered tones of the 'black sheep,' Uncle Harry, and how he ran off with some woman in his red Corvette, never to be seen again.

The political and religious systems want to keep us in debt, guilt, and servitude so that there are still enough "robots" to work the system that ultimately lines their pockets and, in turn, the true bliss of spiritual freedom continues to evade us.

I remember the acute fear I experienced at finding myself out of my body in unchartered territory. Why couldn't I just say, "Wow, this is new. This could be fun!"

No, I fight and shout with my heart beating ninety to the dozen as if my very life is being threatened. That is exactly it. My life as I know it is threatened. And what is more, when the panic is happening, I cannot stop it. This is how deep our fears run. We think we are adventurous. We will bungee jump off tall buildings just to prove it! We are not. We are fearful repetitive creatures where everything we do is measured by its degree of safety.

"We must make the mortgage smaller before we are old, and the house smaller to keep the heating bills down. I will float the company so we have all the money we require for retirement. In fact, I can be a philanthropist so everyone will admire my success and want to be near me. I will never have to face life alone. I must buy medical insurance for when I am sick and life insurance in case I die."

We are content, or not, to get up every day in the same routine, doing the same non-engaging tasks with the same lack of passion so that we can shop for the same food specials that everyone else bought this week, to survive.

How did we become these sad, puny little gnats? In forgetting that we are God, that God lives in us and is all powerful and limitless in its potential, we became afraid of what life could do to us. We fell over and skinned our knees, so now we only wear flat sturdy shoes.

We are supposed to feel pain. It is called living. But we forgot how to clear pain out of our system, how to get up and start anew, wiser for the experience. Instead we carry pain like a great burden until the weight of it is unbearable and we cannot risk any more pain. Now we are afraid of pain, so we will live a safe life.

Within my safety I am now shutting out 80 percent of my creativity, my life force, my passion. My world keeps getting narrower and narrower. I am starting to think smaller, so now I am creating fewer resources, and that makes me feel more afraid.

When I surrendered my fear of the out of body experience, I discovered that I had a heightened sense of awareness that allowed me to access an ecstasy that is rarely reached in three-dimensional matter. I asked, "Why not? Why have I not experienced this before?"

Having had the experience of my light body, I refused to become a working clone of the half-satisfied, half-alive human experience. I began to observe people's level of connectedness to spirit. It showed in their stooped bodies, their tired sighs, despair, and the lines on their faces. Whether they were working class with minimal resources or wearing the finest suit with a six- or seven-figure income, they often shared a similar lackluster life, bogged down by life's demands with a level of dissatisfaction that fueled their addiction for food and/or sex. Suicide was common to both groups.

Nothing in this dimension would ever compare to the soaring free fall of ecstasy I had known as my body floated through the air, twirling unhindered by body mass. Wave upon wave upon wave of pure joy. The intensity of love and unconditional giving exploding colors in my body. I had experienced the freedom of my potential without limitation. I still existed when I was not inside my body. It was not something to believe in at church grappling with the meaning of words like soul and Holy Spirit and concepts of everlasting life. I now knew it. The body was a mere sleeve that could be and would be removed as my life went on.

There was a space we went to, when we were not in a body. Infinite space. Hundreds of millions of entities, life forms, universes, suns giving life to planets—endless possibility. We are so much more than these physical bodies.

The nymphets have never returned, and so the power of their memory has never been diluted and forgotten through repetition. To this day, the experience I had flying through my room while the church bells rang feels as rare and delicious as that Sunday morning when I was twenty-two years old.

8

United States of America: 22 Years Old

Teaching: Ghosts

"Well, why don't you come then," smiled my Louisiana friend.

Bobby had been living, loving, and playing her down-home music here in New Zealand for a few years. She was planning her first trip home to the southern United States of America, and I was asking her all sorts of questions about her homeland.

"Y'all should come. There will be plenty of room in the car from Dallas to Shreveport and my ma and pa will love ya," she insisted.

"Yeah right," I laughed. "Just drop everything and take off to America!"

"Why not? You will love the music, the people, the seafood gumbo. Just use my house as a base and you can travel from there. Southern folk are mighty hospitable and they will welcome you right on into they . . . eer homes," she drawled in her heavy Southern accent.

Bobby was cute with dancing eyes and a rich, mellow singing voice. She could lay down her base and percussion tracks, and with guitar in hand could sing all night with a full band sound. With that accent and bobbing curls, people loved her. I was impressed by entertainers who could pick up the rhythm of any popular tune and soon have a room full of people singing along.

Performing was not my favorite thing to do. I loved to write songs, and being in a recording studio, time stood still. The day I first heard the sound of my voice in a studio, I could not believe it was me.

"It can't be . . . it's well . . . too big."

From that first day, the pure sound from a studio was the most exciting thing on the planet to me. Once recorded and put on tape, it never sounded like that again. The crisp, clear sound within the soundproofed room through the twenty-four-track desk and top-of-the-line speakers pushed the quality of sound into a different orbit. I think I was in love.

A friend and I had laid down some tracks in a professional studio on a shoestring budget. The studio musicians were so impressed with our sound that they offered to donate their time. Wow! That sort of support from top studio musicians who worked daily with bands and some of the country's best vocal talent was very encouraging.

I will always feel grateful to them for the unconditional giving of their time.

I put a copy of my demo tape in my luggage as I packed for the United States of America. I had no idea what I was going to do with it, but you never know. I might meet someone in the music industry.

As promised, Bobby's friend picked us up from the Dallas airport. Her car was the size of a small apartment with huge cow horns bolted to the bonnet. I could not believe my eyes. She sat with the speedometer set at the speed limit, something I had never seen before, and put both boot-clad feet up on the huge bench seat while she chatted and steered with one finger on the endless straight road to Louisiana.

After two weeks, I waved goodbye to Shreveport and took a flight to Houston, Texas. This was how this trip was evolving. I had one phone number for my Houston contact and she had a contact for me in Nashville, Tennessee. Her contact took me down to Baton Rouge, Louisiana, and then on to the west coast of California and San Francisco. I did not stay in one backpacker establishment in over three months. There was a lot to be said for traveling alone. People easily took you into their homes and I was not one to sit around. I would clean the pool, mend the fence, or mix a margarita. I was cheerful, hard working, and easy to have around.

It seemed my "spiritual" experiences were not confined to the shores of New Zealand. I was about to experience something quite extraordinary.

Jackie's house in Houston was large, two-storied, and comfortably air conditioned in the Texas heat with an inviting blue-green swimming pool in the yard.

"In the yard" was such a Southern way of speaking. They all thought I sounded British while I was appalled at how quickly I was falling into lazy, drawn-out vowel sounds. The Southern drawl was catchy. I had this confirmed by my family three months later. The Americans were still calling me British while those at home wanted to know where I got that accent.

It was the first night of my stay at about 3 a.m. Lying in my bed, I heard a steady knocking sound that seemed to be coming from the ceiling. I listened to it for some time and wondered if there was something wrong with the plumbing or perhaps a tree branch was swinging in the wind and hitting the side of the house. I got up to use the bathroom, and from the hallway I heard gentle sobbing coming from Jackie's room. We hardly knew each other and I did not want to intrude on her private grief.

The next morning I was conscious of being extra cheerful. I took some classic photos of 'Jack' floating about in her pool reading the *Wall Street Journal* as she decided which shares to buy, sell, or hold. It was a glorified form of gambling really, but it was the early 1980s before the global crash and there was good money to be made.

The second night was a repeat of the first. I could hear the gentle sobbing from Jackie's room. Should I go to her? I hesitated in the hall. She appeared such a strong, capable woman at least fifteen years my senior. I did not want to embarrass her and slipped back into bed, but I could not sleep. The steady bang, bang, bang from the attic continued. Eventually I dozed off.

As I made Jackie a pot of genuine English Breakfast tea the next morning, a novelty for this coffee-drinking Texan, I asked her, "What is the knocking sound I can hear in the ceiling at night?"

"Tell me about it!" Jackie said with exasperation. "I have had every tradesman you can think of looking for the source of that damn noise. Plumber, gasfitter, and my neighbor who is a builder. We made sure there is nothing growing too close to the house, the gutters are all secure and there is nothing in the loft. It is a real mystery."

My third night in Jackie's house, I lay awake listening to the steady knocking in the ceiling, wondering what on earth it could be. Eventually I got up to get a glass of water. As I passed Jackie's room, I heard deep sniffing and blowing of her nose. I knew she had again been crying. My compassion reached out to her. What had saddened her so?

The door was not latched so I pushed it ajar with a gentle knock.

"Jack?"

"Yes," she answered. Her voice sounded strained and choked up.

"May I come in?"

"Yes," she flicked on her nightlight.

Her eyes were red and swollen as I walked towards the bed.

"I hear you crying every night. Is there anything I can do?"

"No, there is nothing . . . " a tear rolled down Jackie's face.

She looked so deeply sad and vulnerable lying there with the duvet up to her chin.

"Need a hug?" I said, feeling rather foolish.

"That would be nice." Jackie surprised me by pulling back the covers. "Hop in."

I slipped in beside her and wrapped my arms around her as she snuggled her back into me. I just held her as she cried some more and I listened to her breathing change as she fell asleep.

I woke the next day to the smell of pancakes and whistling from the kitchen. I joined Jackie for breakfast and she told me her story.

She had taken a trip to Africa with a woman friend. They had unexpectedly enjoyed a passionate affair on their travels. The friend had made it clear that there was no way it could continue on their return to the States, but poor Jackie had fallen hopelessly in love. She had finally found her perfect partner, and every night she yearned for the love they had shared.

Jackie was particularly cheerful because she hoped a new love was developing with this long-haired beauty from New Zealand. We spoke openly about this and I explained how she was just setting herself up for more heartache. I was leaving in seven days.

"I have a much better idea," I announced. "Take me to every gay club and bar in this town and let's find you a new girlfriend!"

We made a list right then and there of all the qualities Ms. Right had to have.

Available. Attractive. About thirty years old. Independent, but flexible to include Jackie in her life. Good sense of humor and lots of fun. The list went on. Tonight the search would begin.

Sure enough, after a few nights, Jackie had a new love interest. I must say I was quite relieved. I had had my fill of Stetson hats, boots, and wide belt buckles wanting a late night slow dance. Jackie and her new love were soon smitten with each other. I was suddenly spending a lot of my time alone, bobbing around the pool and planning my departure.

It was about 2 a.m. when a small orb of light was radiating through my closed bedroom door. It pulsed a little, growing larger. At first I thought it must be some sort of spotlight shining through the bedroom window. I reached for the curtain, pulling it aside, but the street was in darkness. The orb began to pulsate again and I intuitively knew that it was a visiting spirit.

"Whoa," I exclaimed. "Stop right there! What do you want?"

The light immediately retreated to a much smaller orb of light.

"Okay. That's better."

My heart was racing and I quickly checked to see if I was having one of my out-of-body experiences. Nope, I was definitely awake and fully present. I rubbed the fabric on my duvet cover between my fingers to confirm that I was in the physical dimension.

The light began to enter the room as I conversed with it. I had never experienced any phenomena like this before. I was not in what I called my "between worlds" state and felt the acute fear of the unknown rising.

"Look here, I feel very frightened. Just nice and slow okay?"

The light immediately stilled, just gently pulsing about a meter in diameter and then slowly retreated to about half the size. I felt some immediate relief that this . . . whatever it was . . . seemed to be listening to me and I had some control of the situation.

"Is this really happening?" I asked myself.

I glanced out the window to see the gentle movement of the trees swaying in the breeze under the streetlight. I looked back to the closed door where the light remained constant. Yep, this was really happening.

"Okay, you can come in . . . nice and slow."

I was communicating telepathically without a sound, yet this "being" understood my every thought.

The light grew bigger and brighter until, in what seemed like a moment of unveiling, I was astounded at how bright the whole room was. There was a blinding glare in my eyes like a hot summer day. I clearly heard the words, "Thank you."

"Thank you? What for?" I responded in my mind.

"Thank you" was repeated, and the light began to retreat. Smaller, smaller, little round orb through the door and it was gone.

My body was left with a tingling sensation. I lay in bed digesting the fact that a spiritual being, a consciousness that could understand my thoughts, had just entered my room and spoken to me.

I was, alcohol free—check.

Drug free—check.

Emotionally sane—check.

Awake—check.

It heard me speak with my mind. I heard it speak to me. I was not prone to an overactive imagination. Not in this instance.

I could not wait to tell Jackie the following morning.

As I converted Jackie to more of my English habits, making her crisp toast with marmalade, she began to slowly cry.

"That will be my brother."

Jackie explained that she had been so distraught after returning from South Africa that her kid brother had said he was coming to spend time with her. He was driving overnight from L.A. and would be with her the following day. Instead, Jackie received the news from her tearful mother that Jacob had been involved in a car accident with a semi truck and had died instantly. She blamed herself for his death. She did not have enough room in her aching heart to deal with such pain and woke crying from her sleep every night for a month before my arrival. The steady knocking in the roof had been Jacob still trying to reach his sister to offer her comfort.

With a new love in her life, much of Jackie's natural joy began to return. Jacob gave his thanks that night and the knocking stopped.

Jacob taught me that without our bodies, we still have our emotional field intact.

When "crossing over" to the fifth or sixth dimension after the death of the body, we still have emotions of love, concern, and desire. Emotions that we would label negative, like remorse, jealousy, resentment, and hatred, only exist in the world of duality, which is the third dimension of planet Earth as we know it at this time. The fourth dimension is like a holding zone where spirits get to recoup after a long illness or spend time reviewing their life before moving on. Some spirits are so determined not to let go of their destructive emotions or uncompleted Earthly business that they refuse to move on from the fourth dimension. While in this holding zone, they are removed from the knowingness that they are great, radiant, loving beings and remain entrenched in their petty worldly fights and attachment to worldly possessions or relationships. This is particularly common with sudden death. They may even refuse to believe that they have actually died, and so become incensed when someone moves into *their* house, dates *their* wife, or raises *their* children. Until they move on to a higher frequency of love, they are still capable of negative Earthly emotion, which makes sense of malevolent spirits seeking revenge or those considered ghosts that will not depart this physical world because of emotions like fear and possessiveness.

In Jacob's case, he refused to leave his sister's house until she had healed and received the comfort he had intended to give her. How frustrating it must have felt for him, not to be physically present for her and for Jackie to not realize he was still trying to reach her.

Knowing that we were still emotional beings after death was another milestone in my spiritual understanding. To die hurt, angry, or unresolved in any way means that we carry these emotions with us, in the same way that when we die feeling that we have completed with loved ones and physical possessions, we carry that peace with us.

In the holding zone of the fourth dimension, we are offered healing from higher spiritual beings of love to assist us with unresolved emotion. This does not mean that the emotions miraculously disappear. It requires a willingness to grieve and to forgive to fully release past hurts. The beings that stoically hold on to their pain or how they have been wronged while on Earth bring with them the same clutter in their emotional energy field when they reincarnate. They are usually intent on holding on to the fact that *they are right* and the perpetrator of wrongs against them does not deserve their forgiveness or, through mistakes of their own, they refuse to forgive themselves. The pattern in the field will repeat itself to enable the emotion to become known again, thus giving the being the opportunity to release it, enabling healing to take place. Sadly, most beings become so fixed in physical matter that the repeat of the trauma simply adds another layer to the emotion, insisting that it continues to repeat itself over and over again.

Without the conscious knowledge that we are only hurting ourselves by limiting the rising of our frequency back to the light of love and with the inability to receive direct guidance from higher beings who could remind us who we are, we are like ships cast adrift into the storm without sail or rudder. We really believe that we are the victims of circumstance and our thoughts dwell on the injustice of our demise, which creates more and more of the same.

Hundreds of thousands decide to bail out through suicide as the darkness closes in and they no longer see the light of hope at the end of the tunnel. As the fifth most common cause of death in our teenagers, we as adult educators are completely failing them, by not making the information available to them that they are the God force, the great I AM presence. It is a travesty they are not taught about our collective descent into darkness through the inability to clear the emotional field or discipline negative thoughts. For many, there are now so many layers to their pain that the main energy chakras that distribute the light of spirit to their cells can no longer spin. Joy evades them and physical disease follows.

The spirit has never changed. It is only the inability to experience its beauty that allows the feeling that one is descending into darkness. Just because the day appears grey and raining does not mean that the sun is no longer shining. As the airplane fights its way through thick layers of fluffy clouds, it eventually breaks through to a blinding sun and a clear blue sky. That is you. Radiant. Constant. Refuse to believe the small limited thoughts of a clouded mind and insist upon knowing the truth about your brilliance.

❧ 9 ❧

Nashville, Tennessee: 22 Years Old

Teaching: Fame

Jackie was my stepping stone to Nashville, Tennessee. A friend of hers had a long-distance relationship with a Chicago girl based in Nashville. After assisting Jackie in her time of need, there was nothing this circle of friends wouldn't do for me, and I was welcomed in Tennessee, Florida, and California.

The flight from Houston to Nashville was full. Here I was, off to the music capital of America. I was not a fan of traditional country music, but I knew it floated somewhere in my veins after years of hearing my dad's lovely tenor croon his favorite tunes. "Please release me, let me go, for I don't love you anymore. To waste a life would be a sin . . . release me, and let me, love again . . ."

He would sit in the bottom lounge with his headphones on, listening to the Country Top 40, singing his wee happy face off.

It was not a long flight. I sat directly behind two tall men, both wearing large elaborate belt buckles and Southern cowboy hats. It took me until just before buckling up for landing to build up the courage to stand up and speak with them over their seats.

"Excuse me, are you two men in the music industry?"

"Why honey, how did you know?" they were genuinely impressed.

"Ah . . . something to do with the hats," I wanted to say.

As we talked, their fascination grew as I told them I was from New Zealand. They introduced themselves as the head of Warner Brothers Music and the head of ASCAP, a top publishing house that sold songs to stars all over the world. It took me a few weeks to realize that people came to Nashville from all over America and sang in clubs and bars for years sometimes, with the hope of catching sight of men like this, let alone meeting them. There I was, twenty-two years old, big brown eyes, and thick hair down to my waist with all the naiveté of youth, rattling on about how I had made a demo tape of my own music back in New Zealand.

"Well, sugar, we would love to hear it," they both agreed.

Warner Brothers Music was always looking for the next star and ASCAP was forever hungry to match the next hit song with the right artist.

"I don't think my songs are commercial," I add.

"Can you sing?" asked the Warner Brothers fellow with his deep baritone.

"Yep, no problem there," I stated with confidence.

"We . . eil, you'all be ready, say, 11 a.m.," he drawled, nodding agreement with his friend.

"Give us your address and we . . eil pick you up. Let's have a listen to that tape."

The next morning Barb, my Nashville host, came running back from the front door.

"There is a stretch limo waiting for you!"

"What the . . . ?" The limo filled every available parking space and there stood Mr. ASCAP with the rear door open.

"Why the limo?" I asked incredulously

"Just to see the look on your face, darlin'," he said with a grin. "Welcome to America! You're in the music capital of the world!"

These boys were experts at wooing women. If you didn't have the skills to line their pockets, you were hopefully pretty enough for their sheets. Of course, that did not even cross my mind. My thoughts were all about music!

I was poured a glass of champagne and when we arrived at ASCAP House, the driver was told to continue around the block a few times to give us time to drink it. Mr. ASCAP (I can't remember his name, so this will do) was handsome in a boyish sort of way. He had thick black hair, a smooth face, and was a bit soft around his middle. He had to be at least forty years old to hold such an important position in the company, but he looked youthful and his blue eyes sparkled. Little did I know, that from the moment of our meeting, he felt completely spellbound by this bright chatty Kiwi girl. He had tried to push the feelings away by telling himself that I was far too young and that he had a steady girlfriend.

We walked into the foyer of ASCAP House with its gleaming tiles and ornate sculptures. Mr. ASCAP led the way down the hallway to his palatial office. There were photos all over the walls. One with his arm wrapped around Dolly Parton and another standing with a big smile between both Dolly and Kenny Rogers. They were celebrating an award for the hit song "Islands in the Stream."

"Take a seat." He pointed to a black leather chair sitting nearby while he sat in a large swivel chair on the far side of his huge ornate wooden desk.

He had my New Zealand demo tape in his hand and plugged it in to his tape deck. He slowly turned his chair until he had his back to me, leaning back to listen to my recording through the finest sound system available.

My song began,

"Living is for loving.
To live without love, we really have nothing at all.
Having is to have given.
If to have is to hold, when do we learn how
     to share?
Honesty is to believe in.
To believe in a lie, the truth will never be found.

What will be the fated future of our kingdom?
Do we just turn around and watch the castle
     fall down?
In a world full of madness,
Searching for goodness in all mankind . . .
Searching their eyes . . .
It is up to us, to have the final say.
In the way that we live, in the way that we spend
     our days.
I see the heartache of the suffering child.
I see the madness of the crazy mind
In this world full of sadness,
Searching for goodness in all mankind.
Searching their eyes . . .
. . . to live without love, we really have nothing at
     all."

I cringed as he listened to the very first song I had ever written at the grand age of eighteen years old. It had no winning formula, hook lines, or chorus crescendo, just the raw emotion of one who could see. I felt suddenly vulnerable and naïve that anyone in Mr. ASCAP's position would be the slightest bit interested in my songs. I felt myself flushing with embarrassment that here I was sitting amongst the photos of the country music legends and that this man of such importance had gone to such effort to pick me up. It was embarrassing to be wasting his time.

Even with these thoughts I felt a stirring of pride for my song. I knew in a city like Nashville my songs of political and social injustice would be cast aside but I liked it.

I had managed against all odds to produce a professional recording with some great musicians who believed in me.

The song came to an end and I held my breath. The chair slowly turned and Mr. ASCAP looked me right in the eye.

"Honey . . . I can make you a star."

The room was silent. Did he really just say that? I was speechless. He continued, "Your songs ain't gonna make it here in Nashville, but your voice . . . extraordinary. And just look at you honey. You are so beautiful. You are the whole package. And that voice!"

His excitement was clearly building as he started talking very animatedly. "You have such power in your voice. You could be 'country rock.' You would be great with ballads. You are not a straight country singer. Did you know we are into all sorts of crossovers now, country blues, country pop . . . we need to get you into a studio to demo various crossovers and see what best suits your voice. Johnny from Warner is gonna wanna hear this. We might just wait until we have a combination demo and then just knock his socks off. If he don't want you, I will see Glen at Sony or Billy Jean at Universal. Man, she would just love you. I know for a fact that she is lookin for a new powerhouse female vocalist...God damn, they're gonna be queuing up to sign your pretty face . . ."

He stopped to come up for air. He was striding up and down his office by now.

"Do you know how hard it is to get someone to pay for the studio time?" He kept vocalizing everything that was rushing through his mind.

"You see, that's the hardest thing. If I take them a top demo, I know they gonna want ya, cause they're not gonna understand that New Zealand demo of yours. But how to get the record company to put money on the table before they've even heard ya? . . . That's the sticking point and I haven't got it in my budget to do that. I tell you what . . . I'm gonna find the right songs. I don't care if it takes all night and I'm gonna bring them to you tomorrow morning for you to learn. You just practice them and I will find a way to get you into a studio."

"Damn, I'll pay for it myself," he muttered under his breath.

"Come on now. Let me take you to lunch. We have a lot to talk about."

"My God girl! You're good!" he exclaimed as he grabbed his Stetson off the hook by the door.

I don't know what strings Mr. ASCAP pulled or whether anyone even knew we were in the studio. All I know was that three days after our initial meeting, he told me to be ready by midnight.

Apart from one lone sound technician, the studio was in darkness. When you did a demo tape in Nashville, the song writer had already recorded all the instruments, lead vocal, and harmonies. It was only a matter of replacing the lead vocal track with my voice, which is what I had practiced in the bedroom of Barb's tiny flat. That was the only room with air conditioning.

Mr. ASCAP was in a bit of a fluff because he couldn't find the master recording of one of the songs he had chosen. He wanted one ballad, one standard country, and one country rock song to fully test my voice.

"I will have to go upstairs and hunt for it. Shouldn't be long." He jumped the stairs two at a time.

That left me and the sound technician waiting while the backing track ran.

"Let's do a take while we wait," I suggested.

I entered the soundproof booth and there was that gorgeous purity of sound that only a studio had. I had rehearsed the song over and over again so at its completion I said, "Yep, happy with that. Let's run the next one."

Mr. ASCAP arrived back in the studio in time to hear the second song completed as I added a few extra harmonies. I had put my stamp on both songs, which were sounding quite different from the originals. Not only could he not believe what had been achieved in one take, he loved the different sound of what he called my "British voice." He was thrilled, for the sooner we could get out of the studio the better he said. I semi expected to hear the crack of an angry voice saying, "What the hell are you doing in here?"

I asked no questions. The master he had searched for was "The Bed You Made for Me."

The title gives a clue as to its content, sung by the writer with a strong southern drawl.

"This is a great little song that has been on my books for six years now. I can't understand why nobody has bought it," Mr. ASCAP exclaimed.

In my rehearsal, I had completely changed the song by removing the southern drawl that I could not possibly do and stay true to myself. The song was crying out for some strong harmonies, which I added and wow, it sounded great!

"That's a hit song you got there!" Mr. ASCAP was excited.

"Just one thing. I don't expect a southern accent from you, but you can't say 'satin sheets.' It's sah . . . in. Soft on the T. Rolling . . . sah . . . in."

No "t" sound allowed in country music, so I said run it again . . . and again. That "t" just snuck in there, and again and again.

"Okay! We have the British version of sa . . .tin sheets." Mr. ASCAP laughed and let it go.

It was four months after this night when back in New Zealand, that my friend sent me a recording by a top Nashville band, Highway 101. "The Bed You Made for Me" peaked at number 4 on the Hot Country Songs charts after sitting on the shelf unrecorded for six years. My demo had sold the song for ASCAP. The band had even kept some of my harmony arrangements, so I was pretty chuffed.

The next two weeks in Nashville was a whirlwind of meet and greet. People in the industry wanted to meet the girl behind the sound and Mr. ASCAP wanted me to meet everyone! We socialized all over Nashville as I was introduced to all the right music people, wined and dined with the head of this and the head of that. I didn't take much notice of who was who and totally trusted Mr. ASCAP to be looking out for my interests. Why wouldn't he? They were all hungry for the next star, the next hit. One hit song could make everyone a lot of money. I remember learning that the songwriter could earn as much as the singer and I thought, 'Now there's a go. Make the same money, live the same lifestyle without having to be the face up front.' There was something really appealing about that.

During this time, I listened to some of the finest live performances in small cafes and bars all over town. I would say to Mr. ASCAP, "She can really sing! Why don't they record her?"

He would answer, "Because she is a dime a dozen, nothing unique. Sounds like everybody else. What they love about you is that you are different."

I was also high risk. I had very little live performance experience and had no existing crowd following. Back at this time, the early 1980s, you had to travel and perform to promote the album to achieve sales. There was no YouTube or Internet, and video recordings were just beginning and pretty basic.

It was decided that while Mr. ASCAP pursued a record deal, I would return to New Zealand to pack up the apartment I rented, which overlooked the lights of Auckland City and the Harbour Bridge. Life was good and I loved my homeland, but hey . . . America wouldn't be forever.

Mr. ASCAP invited me to his apartment for a farewell dinner. He said he was cooking something special in my honor. He sent a cab for me and upon arrival I realized he had planned a cozy night, just the two of us. Over a glass of wine he confessed that he had fallen in love with me and how much he had tried for it not to happen because of his long-standing relationship. The reality was that Mr. ASCAP had never experienced a girl *not* sleeping with him to get ahead in her music career and my carefree friendship had allowed his affections to blossom. I tried to explain that I was incredibly fond of him, loved his company, but did not feel the same way. He was having real trouble taking no for an answer as he steered me towards the bedroom.

Saved by the bell. His doorbell.

There stood his girlfriend.

"You wanna tell me what's going on!?" she demanded, hands on hips with her Farrah Fawcett blond locks swinging and her wee cowboy boots tapping.

I knew straight away. I did not want to mess with her. She was as tough as he was soft and was probably raised riding wild bulls and such.

"It's not what you think," Mr. ASCAP stammered, trying to find the right holes for his shirt buttons.

Her anger was rising and her flushed face was bright pink. I had visions of her shouting, "Yee . . . ha" and slapping some poor animal's flank. It was time to step in.

"Honestly nothing was going to happen here tonight. We are friends. And nothing is *ever* going to happen between us."

Mr. ASCAP looked at me with the confusion of a hurt puppy on his face. He sank into the couch with an expression that went from total disbelief to genuine pain.

"I will get a cab. You two enjoy dinner and I will see you in three months. Thanks for everything." I walked toward Mr. ASCAP and bent down to hug him. I quietly spoke into his ear, "I am so sorry. I did not know how you felt."

He squeezed me like he never wanted to let me go. Grief etched on his face. I kissed his cheek and left him to face the music with the "cattle rustler" as I made a speedy exit.

During my month home I ran into a New Zealand music icon in the supermarket. He asked me what I had been up to and I told him about the Nashville experience. It just so happened that he was hosting a country television show that was sold to the Nashville Network Television and played on local TV in America twice a week in exchange for starring American artists on the show.

"I would love to hear that demo," he said enthusiastically.

We drove to the studio there and then and within the week I had a contract offer on my desk asking me to join the cast of the TV show for one year.

I rang Mr. ASCAP to ask him what I should do. He was ecstatic.

"Do you know how hard it is to get on American television!? Just about impossible; that's how hard. By doing the show, you'll be in people's living rooms and they will all know who you are before your record is released. There ain't no better news for your career."

There was no sign of his disappointment or possible relief that I was not returning as planned. He was a professional businessman who knew I needed all the help I could get to score a recording contract. Music was an expensive business and for every artist that made them millions in sales there were a hundred mistakes that cost them dearly. Top executives had to be certain of enough success to recoup costs or risk losing their lucrative position in the company. And let's face it, the kudos, the travel, the hotels, the women . . . it was hard to let go of once you had reached the top of your game.

The days on the television set were long and drawn out as I waited my turn for dress rehearsal and sound check. The performance was live to air and totally nerve-wracking. Any mistake and everyone would see it, including Nashville. I did not want to seem ungrateful for such an opportunity, but I was both anxious and bored out of my brain. This was considered the cream of my career. Paid airfares, fancy hotels, and restaurants with excited fans asking for your autograph at the end of a show, and I was barely tolerating it. What was wrong with me? I yearned to return to the excitement of Nashville and my love of the recording studio. There was talk about the girl who had recorded in Nashville and was heading back there so I received quite a bit of the silent attitude, "And who the hell are you? Newcomer Hot Shot!"

I remember one woman tapping the star on her door to get my attention as she asked me to move on in the hallway. I was crowding her space.

EMI Records NZ got wind of things and produced a single with me, with the desire to make an album. Songs were arriving from Nashville thick and fast as I worked to choose songs to record. There were so many I didn't want. Well, most of them actually. There were radio interviews, the *Women's Weekly* magazine and a performance in the Michael Fowler Centre in Wellington as they presented me with the award for "Most Promising Female Vocalist of the Year." It was 1984 and I was twenty-four years old.

I had achieved in three short weeks in Nashville what many singers had dreamed of for years and attempted with failure. I did not enjoy performing. One day I sat down and had a really good think about what I wanted.

I thought, if I am only just tolerating this, what is it going to be like back in America having to perform? Mr. ASCAP said he was getting close to securing a recording contract with one condition: that I would have to promote the album sales by traveling in a bus with a band the length and breadth of America. A dream come true for some. A total nightmare for me.

I honestly couldn't think of anything I would enjoy less. Perhaps studying ingrown toenails or the secret sex life of a sea anemone.

I loved writing songs. I could start a song in the morning and work at it all day until I was happy that it was complete. It would suddenly be 3 p.m. and I had not eaten, fingers swollen from the guitar strings, and I had lost all sense of time. Writing songs taught me about the passion of creativity in the present where time no longer existed.

It suddenly dawned on me that since the whirlwind of Nashville and the constant listening to Nashville-based songs for recording and television performances, I had not written one song in more than two years. I had gone from a prolific creative writer to nothing after being told my songs were not commercially viable. I felt a deep grief and realized that even though my songs did not follow a successful formula for three-minute radio songs, my greatest love was creating music. I knew that I would never be happy performing other peoples' songs on stage.

These realizations came about at the same time that EMI made another budget cut to the album I was to record in New Zealand. I was unknown, high risk, and they were getting cold feet. I was working with New Zealand's top producer and he gave me the news that we no longer had a string section for the album.

"I am not sure I want to put my name to this," he said. "There have been too many cuts to make a quality product."

This was the out that I needed.

"Well, if it is not good enough for your name, it is not good enough for mine," I said.

That was it. The TVNZ contract was complete, the bus journey to every club and bar in America felt like an impossibility, and I walked away.

There is always a hollow place when one journey ends and the next has not begun. My spiritual studies told me at the time that energetically if you changed direction while in the midst of success, you would take that energy into the next activity.

I not only had to quell my own fears as to whether I had done the right thing, but endured the disbelief of family and friends alike. One musician was very angry.

"Do you know how that makes me feel? You were handed everything I have ever dreamed of and you just shrug it off as not what you want!"

Or, "You are a wonderful singer. It is such a waste."

It was true that what I had been offered was exceptionally rare and I could be seen to be wasting my talent, but performing in smoky bars was not part of my dream. I realized that most people would put up with just about anything to achieve *fame* when I couldn't think of anything worse and saw it as a distraction to my inner spiritual journey. I imagined walking into a restaurant with everyone staring, pointing, or wanting my autograph with all anonymity gone. I cringed at the thought.

I faced a very hard lesson in being true to myself and refused to be identified by something I did rather than who I AM. What others thought was none of my business, and I had to search deep within myself to ask myself, what was my passion?

The human race, including myself, rising off their knees and awakening to our greatest potential. I knew my music could entertain and even bring great happiness to people, but it couldn't fulfill that passion. Within moments of making my decision to follow my true passion, my world as a spiritual healer unfolded.

How often have you been socializing in a room of people where both yourself and others are quick to make assumptions about those present?

"I would like you to meet Maria Phillips. She is the Head Consultant of Paediatrics at St. Margarets."

"Hello, nice to meet you," I said, deciding I should look suitably impressed.

"Maria, meet Meryl Yvonne. She too has a medical background and runs her own very successful healing practice. I recommend her to everyone! You too specialized in pediatrics didn't you, Meryl?"

Already I am wondering if Maria is anything like the arrogant consultant I experienced as a student nurse and Maria is thinking, 'Specialized? A nurse I suppose. Her own healing practice? Hmm . . . one of those alternative people.'

"Please excuse me," Maria apologizes. "I have just spotted Charmaine from obstetrics and I have a matter I need to discuss with her."

We all make judgments and assumptions about people all the time because of what they *Do*, not who they *Are*. I am not identified by what I do.

A man walks a little taller with his chest pumped a little further because he just made the Rich List.

"I am wealthy. I am successful, so I am important and intelligent."

No. You have succeeded at what you *Do*, which brought wealth into your life. As for feeling important, that is the trap of the ego that has identified the self as *I am what I do or am seen doing*.

As for intelligent?

Have you ever noticed the strange phenomenon whereby someone who comes by wealth suddenly assumes that they are more intelligent than others? Their delusions of self-importance suddenly elevate their cerebral capacity. This is a great example of ego in motion. There are, of course, wealthy people with fine aptitude, however they are not synonymous.

"I am a famous actress."

That is not who you are. One of your talents is acting, which is why they gave you the job. Lots of people enjoyed the movie, which is why they now know you by name.

There is nothing at all wrong with succeeding at what you *do*; loving what you *do*. Just don't make the mistake of believing that that is who you *are*. Ultimately it will confine you and limit you to your career, your country, your politics, your race, your age, religion, social standing, likes, dislikes, and all you identify with. That is not who you *are*.

When I do not identify with what I *do*, I am left with the question, 'Who am I?'

What I AM is the *energy* that propels me to the success. I am not the success itself, nor can I be the failure. In understanding that I am energy or spirit first and foremost, I can co-create with that energy by directing my intention into anything I choose to manifest without limitation.

It is the focus of your energy that enabled you to pass the bar and now you practice law. To identify as being a lawyer traps you in the limitation of your salary and the wealth of possessions that surround you, your colleagues who you identify as your friends and the clubs and restaurants you frequent, your sense of pride as you serve your community, your politics that are right as you fight injustice. All of these things may be real and important in your life, but they still limit you. Your I AM has no limits.

Ko au te maunga.
Ko au te awa.
Ko au te moana.
Ko nga rakau oku tuakana.
Ko au te Ngahere.

I am the mountain.
I am the river.
I am the ocean.
The trees are my older siblings.
I am the Forest.

When I awaken to the knowledge that I am a part of all that is, I am limitless. I have no boundaries. I am not a great singer that could be famous. That is something I could choose to pursue or not. It is not who I AM.

Who I am does not change no matter what I do.

By releasing potential, fame and fortune I was left with the empty slate of nothingness where there was only my I AM presence. In this space, I no longer needed people's approval, opinions, or acceptance.

I was free. Pure potential.

∾ 10 ∾

Only One Chance: 23 Years Old

Teaching: Focus

What a magnificent day. A hot sun reflected off the white shimmering sands of Mangawhai Heads Beach and the ocean glistened with beckoning welcome. I had joined a gathering of local musicians on a farm nearby and a group of about twelve of us walked the dusty road down to the coast. By the time we kicked off our shoes and stretched our toes in the silken sand, we felt more than ready to cool off in that delicious-looking water. The waves were breaking a long way off shore. I could see a smattering of surfers way out the back waiting for the perfect ride.

Being a hardy Northern girl, I had grown up on the coast and had spent many hours body surfing waves at Matapouri Bay with my father. We especially loved it after a storm when we would tackle a ten-foot swell and thought nothing of being tossed, rolled, or slammed into the sand. It was all part of the fun. We had to be very fit and would return to the bach bedraggled and exhausted.

It would be a good swim out to where the waves were breaking, but I did not hesitate.

"I'm off for a body surf. See you soon," I called to my friends.

No one else was keen to venture out and they happily waved me goodbye. I swam well out over my head and immediately caught a few good rides. There was a stiff offshore breeze, so the waves were a lot bigger when I got up close to them. They packed quite a punch, but nothing I was unfamiliar with and the rides were exhilarating.

One of my friends had been watching me with great admiration and I waved out at the end of a good ride and began the return swim to where the waves were breaking. I could see the waves peeling off beautifully for some of the surfers out the back. I had given surfing a go when I was fifteen years old, but found the board a hindrance compared to the freedom of diving under the waves, and I loved the feeling of my body slicing through the water at high speed.

As I raised my head after a good swim to the deeper water, I was confronted with a wall of water at least twelve feet tall. It was arching, ready to break, and I knew my best bet was to dive under it rather than get caught up and tossed about by its white water. This wave was way too big to catch and could easily smash me into the sand. I did not fancy a broken neck, or anything else for that matter, so I took a deep breath and prepared to dive. I had to dive deep as the wave had a strong undertow. As I surfaced, there was the next wave, exactly the same.

'Bloody close set,' I was thinking as I dived again.

I surfaced to find the next wave almost on top of me. It was huge, towering above me. The wind had increased and the waves were suddenly bigger. To be tumbled by a wave this size would not be pleasant in the least, and at most I could be seriously injured. I had no choice but to get underneath it. Again, I had to dive deep. I came up to see the next wave and at least three more behind it, two of them bigger still.

"Okay, this is number four. The set should only have seven or eight waves and I will be through them." I coached myself to remain calm.

Between the depth of the dive, surfacing, and diving again, I only just had enough time to gasp as much air as possible, which never seemed enough. My lungs were burning and I was tiring fast.

Number eight began to curl above me.

"This is it, you can do it," and I dived again.

The hook of the wave grabbed at my legs and threatened to suck me backwards. No way! I knew that I did not have enough air in my lungs to withstand the lengthy tumble in a wave this big. I pulled at the water with both arms and kicked hard and I was under the wave. As I surfaced, the sea was calm. I was through the set. My body felt limp with exhaustion. I was a long way off shore, and it was certainly time to make my way back.

It was then that I saw it. Coming from the back with the surfers floating over their towering peaks came the next set of huge waves. I knew I didn't have it in me to get through them. I quickly raised my arm and called out as loud as I could to indicate to the surfers or anyone on the beach that I was in trouble. A couple of my friends thought I was waving to them and merrily waved back. The surfers were too far away to hear me and had their boards facing out to sea. They too needed to keep their wits about them in such high seas.

"This could be it. I could drown here today."

I just knew I could not get through the waves that marched ominously towards me. I ached longingly for the shore and to feel my feet on solid ground. I needed a miracle.

And there she was. My little miracle. A smaller wave about half the size leading the set. I had to catch that wave. It was my only chance.

"Okay, kid. There are no second chances here. You have to catch that wave in the exact right spot and take it all the way to shore. You can do it. You know exactly what to do. Now focus!"

I did not take my eyes off that wave for a moment. I watched it steadily growing and taking on its shape ready to break. To get to the wave too soon would be to miss the ride and be left with the huge set of waves behind it growing taller with every moment. To catch it too late would mean moving toward shore in the white water, but not far enough.

"Take your time. Be calm . . . move out! Out! Out! Swim, swim!"

I had to catch the full curl of the wave as I raced to position myself. There was no sandy bottom to push myself off of, as the water was too deep. My position had to be perfect.

"Now! Now! Swim hard!"

I felt the familiar liftoff as my body went over the curl of the wave. With both arms outstretched and head tucked to my chest, I leaned hard to the right, soaring through the water. I lifted my head with immense relief as I rocketed down the face of the wave.

"You beauty, you beauty."

As the wave stopped its perfect shapely peel, I crashed down into a twisting, turning, frothing white water. My body rolled as water was forced up my nose and the sickly taste of sea water ran down my throat. It eventually spat me out and I felt tears of relief as I felt the sand under my feet. My vision blurred, I could see people laughing and clapping in celebration of such a great ride.

I tried to stand and could not. All strength had left my legs and I crawled as best I could.

I felt hands reaching for me and the dragging of my heels in the sand as I saw faces suddenly sober.

All I could manage was, "I wasn't waving."

With my life depending on it, I did not take my *focus* off the wave that I needed to catch. It was my one-pointed determination without distraction that saved my life that day. Even with tremendous odds stacked against me, manifestation was able to occur. I imagined catching the smaller wave in the exact right place and saw it in my mind's eye taking me all the way to safety.

Imagine if I could take that level of focus into everyday activities. I could manifest anything! No one had ever said to me, "Master how to hold your focus without distraction and that which you focus on must manifest. In fact, it is the law of this dimension. If you deem it to be so, so it is."

In fact, if we were to hold *only* positive, focused thought, that is all that would occur! Until we began having duality of thought, good/bad, right/wrong, love/hate, and so forth, that is all that did occur, for millions of years.

This truth hit me like a thunderbolt. All I had read about ancient times in history on the lands of Mu and Atlantis where people like the Lemurians lived for thousands of years in peace and harmony began to make sense. No poverty, no disease or disharmony. Without the collection of negative energy in the energy field, our bodies were made up of a higher frequency of light matter, so that we lived for hundreds of years. We completed mastery in co-creation with physical matter before ascending (taking our light body with us) back to the higher frequency of the fifth and sixth dimensions.

We have fallen so far in our consciousness since then that it is almost impossible to comprehend that when we only had thoughts of love and peace, that is all we manifested. This is at the heart of the original story of Adam and Eve. It was not until Eve (representing the feminine energy of pure thought) "tasted" the thought of opposites, Good *and* Evil, that negativity could manifest. With the power of free will gifted to us in this dimension to be co-creators, we have 'run-amuck' ever since. The more negativity we vibrate with the more karmic debt we accumulate, the more negativity we experience, and so it goes on and on. The destructive thoughts and emotions infiltrate our cellular structure, which we carry as disease from one lifetime to another and one generation to another. It then impregnates the molecular structure of the planet itself, which creates adverse weather conditions, earthquakes, volcanic eruptions, and so on. If you say to most people that it is our inability to be at peace individually that creates all chaos on Earth, they would not contemplate this as truth. They are so convinced that they are victims of circumstance, placing God outside themselves as a separate entity, and then despair at how God can allow such catastrophic events causing such pain and suffering. The suffering will not change until we realize that the spark of God is within each of us.

When we individually take responsibility for experiencing only love and giving in our lives, mastering discipline over unruly detrimental emotions, our planet will know peace.

The law of manifestation does not hold judgment as to whether it is a good or a bad thought. It just is. If every day you focus on the injustice of your work environment, the guy who started a year after you will beat you to the promotion you deserve.

If every day as you open the bills you experience the emotion of gratitude that you are fortunate enough to have a job that pays all your bills, the work gets more inspiring and the bank deposits keep coming. It really is just where we put our *focus*.

I had heard my elders speaking of having the right attitude. Now I understood why. As I stated, "I am bored" with the accompanying deep sigh, I would soon have the feeling of lethargy and disinterest.

My Great Aunt would say to me, "There is no such thing as boredom, just a lack of imagination."

As I contemplated this statement, I would immediately begin to imagine what I could be doing and, sure enough, boredom did not exist. So if I could only hold positive, loving, peaceful thoughts, my world would be full of joy, love, and peace, and lack of enthusiasm would not exist? I needed to become the observer of my thoughts, to be more conscious of what I was thinking.

I was reading a book that talked about the phenomena of "wandering mind" when practicing meditation. Within five breaths, no matter how hard we try to focus, the mind will wander. One moment I am practicing the complete relaxation of my legs in meditation so that I can direct my focus. The next thing my mind has wandered to the kitchen trying to remember if I got the log of dog food out of the freezer. That leads to the image of the little pieces of wire tying the ends of the log, which is why I can't thaw it in the microwave . . . which is why it is important to remember if I took it out of the freezer. . . . Why don't they use plastic ties so they can go in the microwave? . . . I supposed they are pressure packed and might not be strong enough. . . . It really disturbs me to see that look on Marama's face when she is really hungry and I have nothing to feed her. . . . I suppose the chickens are hungry too. . . . I need more chicken food. . . . I will get it when I go to town. . . . Which day am I going to town? . . . It can't be tomorrow as I am meeting that man who will trim the hedge. . . . Did he say that he was $35 per hour? . . .

What is this inane babble in my brain!? These are called *chains of thoughts*. One thought leads to another. From relax your legs and slow your mind, to dog food, packaging, hunger, trip to town, and the hedge all in about fifteen seconds. . .

The constant chatter in the brain is dispersing energy to the kitchen, the freezer, outside to the hedge, to the past, and to the future. Nowhere near my legs! Speed that up by half and I can call it *anxious*. Double it and I am suffering from *stress*. Double the speed again and I *can't think straight*. I could be losing my mind. Rev it a bit more and, "Doctor, I *am* losing my mind."

Pills, numbness, disconnection. Legs? What legs?

When I know my mind has wandered, I am back in the moment and the wandering has stopped. When my mind is doing one of its undisciplined world tours without my permission, linking chain after chain, I am not even aware that it is happening! I get little hints like, "The keys are no longer in the ignition so I must have brought them inside, but where did I put them down? It was *me* that put them down. So where was I?"

In some petty waste of space chain in my brain. That's where!

I have just walked into this room and have no recollection as to what it was I came to get. And no, it is not a sign of my brain aging with early dementia. It is my mind's thoughts moving so fast that I am already up to next week and the task in the room is today.

I hear people complain that these wandering events seem to increase as they get older. It is possible as the brain gets older it is not as efficient, hence going over endless things to remember in different time zones. It is possible too that we just have more to think about. It used to be as simple as what to wear Saturday night and that person is very attractive. Now it's a senior position in the office with the needs of ten other staff members directly receiving your guidance, full management of the house and accounts, not only the ongoing concerns for children, but all those grandchildren, my partner's health issues and my own, and I must remember to bake cookies for the neighbor because her sister just died and Mom is getting to old for ladders and will need my help in the orchard. It seems to be stacked against us, the older we get. Wandering mind? More like a trapeze act while youthful wee Johnny seems only to have to think about his imaginary sword. No wonder he giggles while I sigh with furrowed brow. His mind is ticking slow enough to fully engage in one singular fantasy while I do not know what to tackle next.

So it seems, the more responsibility we have, the more we have to "worry" about. If worry is to have undisciplined thoughts about the future, then that was where my mind just wandered. The more my mind wanders, the more I do not deliver successfully in present time, so the more my thoughts include 'could have, would have, should have,' and I am now wandering into the past. If all joy lives in the moment, no wonder I am still not smiling while Johnny is having a ball!

It is up to me to become conscious of *focus*. I have to train myself to slow the mind, and at the same time discipline my thoughts to be positive, optimistic, and loving if I want positive outcomes in my life. I find this to be near impossible in my everyday state of consciousness with life's numerous distractions. I have to become totally silent, totally still with my body completely heavy as if asleep yet my mind still alert. This is not enough in itself, for the mind can continue its busy rampage as it enters the dream state until I am completely asleep. I have to give the mind simple tasks and be satisfied that I am successfully slowing it down and stopping the meaningless chains of thought that can spread like a virus in a split second.

I observe the in breath and then shift the focus to the out breath, taking care to not let any task continue for more than five breaths; watch the circle of breath; feel the in breath cool in the nostrils breathing in and warm breathing out; watch the rise of the chest, the fall of the chest.

I focus my mind on the farthest sound I can hear and then the closest incessant chirp of a bird. I listen for "Cosmic sound" like a high-pitched singing in my ears. The Masters called it the beating of a thousand beetle's wings. I hear it loud and clear, like crickets singing in the summer. Once I have identified the sound, I am aware it has always been there, it has never left me, and sometimes in the still silence of the night it is almost deafening.

I work with colors in different parts of my body. Blues and violet in the upper centers descending into green, yellow and the orange/reds of earth. I spend time humming and sounding different frequencies of vibration into my body and slowly I train the mind to slow down.

As the mind slows with concentrated focus, the most remarkable experiences begin to happen. I realized that I am staying present with my body rather than darting "hither and thither" through thought. In this present time, joy bubbles up from deep inside my body and often I cannot suppress the laughter. There is nothing specific to laugh about, just a great sense of happiness. Is this why babies can just coo and smile for hours in their cots as long as they are dry and fed?

My body that was initially heavy and relaxed through focus begins to get lighter and lighter until it matters not whether I can feel it at all. Using my mind I can imagine myself rising to the ceiling and there I am. I am awake but free of my body. I get more adventuresome and float above the house or practice scooting sideways at the speed of light. Anything I hold my focus on I can do. If I want to return to an Earthly task, I just imagine where my hands and feet are and again feel the heaviness of my body ready to stretch and awaken.

I am familiar with dissociative states due to drugs, alcohol, or emotional trauma whereby the body is somewhat numb to the senses. This is completely different. The disassociation from the body is because of the intense focus on being present so that other higher-frequency senses are awakened instead of the denser bodily frequencies. In this state I can hear celestial bells, smell the scent of sweet perfume, and sometimes hear a voice with a simple message. I can see brilliant colors and sometimes what is like a kaleidoscope of rolling pictures. They move so quickly I have trouble seeing what they mean. I learn to slow them down as those in spirits communicate with me more easily through imagery. This is meditation. To practice it is to touch upon the essence of our true nature that is all joy and all wisdom.

I do not have to create my happiness or study to be wise; that in my true nature—I am this already. We all are. We just have to learn to be still enough to tap into that which we have always been. The rest of it, the busy mind, the endless tasks of a busy schedule is the illusion. There is nothing wrong with dancing the dance, playing the game of life within the illusion, as long as we remember it is exactly that, a creative illusion.

A higher frequency of light, joy, and peace is my true essence, the energy of the God force flowing through me. It is how I arrived and how I will leave this dimension with the illusion crumbling dust, blowing in the wind.

We have been fortunate to have some great teachers walk the Earth. Dig a little, and much of the knowledge is there.

Christ said, "All things whatsoever you ask in prayer, believing, you shall receive." (Matthew 21:22) "And I say unto you, Ask, and it shall be given you; seek, and ye shall find; knock, and it shall be opened unto you." (Luke 11:9)

Isaiah said, "So shall my word be that goeth forth out of my mouth: it shall not return unto me void, but it shall accomplish that which I please, and it shall prosper *in the thing* whereto I sent it." (Isaiah 55:11)

Whatever I could imagine already exists. I did not have to create success, wealth, love, or anything else that I wanted manifest. Success, wealth, and love already existed.

I needed to become the *frequency* of success, wealth, and love through *focus* so that I could experience them.

The ideal was not to spend one's life in meditation, but to take the teachings of meditative focus and apply them to life. With focus I could manifest anything at all.

As I discussed my near drowning with friends, someone made the comment, "You were damn lucky you caught that wave."

That is exactly how most of us think. We are perpetual victims of circumstance. Lucky or unlucky. Tossed to and fro at the whim of others; at the hands of a punishing God outside of ourselves, depending upon whether we have sinned or not? Whoever dreamed up that story had plans to control the world through the fear generated in its people! The fact is, if I believe I have sinned and that hell and damnation will rain down upon me, my thoughts are so powerful that they allow the punishment to begin. My misery and misfortune is now proof that God is indeed angry with me.

Anything we think about, any words we state, will begin to manifest. It is the law of the God-Force in motion in this dimension. Any teacher, guru, healer, or clergyman that does not teach you that *you* are the master of your reality is not the genuine article or lives in the shadow of his or her own ignorance. The all-powerful creative energy that is God is in me and in you; it is in the mountains, trees, rivers, and every creature of the Earth. Without the God-Force, they could not be manifest.

When I held the intense focus of my thoughts upon catching the wave without wavering, the God-Force was set in motion in me. If God was the ocean, the wave, and the shore and God was also me; we were one and the same in that moment. I was the wave, I was the shore. My body arriving on the shore had to happen for I had deemed it to be so.

"When you can see things already perfect and complete in Divine mind, your clarity of vision pierces the world of matter." (I AM Discourses by the ascended Master, St. Germain)

People catch their manifested waves to shore every day. This realization felt like it brought huge freedom into my life. Life was no longer happening to me, good or bad. I was happening to my life!

It was not my realization that freed my life. I was already free. The wisdom was already me. My experience brought me into the frequency of the knowing.

❦ 11 ❦

Eyes of the Children: 26 Years Old

Teaching: Support

I sat watching the flow of the creek weave its way around the rocks and young ferns. I was beginning to feel the dampness of the grassy riverbank through my trousers. I loved the smell of the earth. It was nice to take a little time outdoors after a busy morning in my healing clinic. I chuckled to myself, remembering the last session. As I put a little traction on my client's neck, she let out a gasp as energy cascaded through her twitching body and all the glasses in the cabinet began to rattle.

"What the . . .?"

I had seen a sudden flow of energy move many a body, but not inanimate objects! It took me a moment to realize that Wellington was having one of its small earthquake tremors.

It had been a little joyous entertainment in a rather sober day. I just felt down and couldn't seem to shake it. Self pity does that to you.

"Where is everyone else?" I complained bitterly to whoever in the spirit world cared to listen.

I had one pair of hands and people were booking in three months in advance. Everyone seemed to need two or three two-hour sessions to clear the clutter in the etheric field to get the main chakras (energy wheels) spinning. If there had been a lot of childhood trauma, they needed even longer. How was this helping to raise the consciousness of the planet? It seemed so slow. We needed an army of workers to make a dent in the mess out there, to clear the accumulated blockages in people's energy fields so that they had any chance of remembering who they really were.

Great powerful beings of light! Instead, they traipsed through my clinic with their various physical ailments, caught up in twisted dysfunctional emotions; many yearning to be free but not knowing how.

It took me a while to realize the "web effect" of my work. The day I asked to work with the light workers, I began to see how they in turn worked more efficiently and had a greater healing effect within society. I spent my time assisting and realigning the energy of doctors and other health professionals, natural healers, politicians, journalists, company C.E.O.s, filmmakers, performing artists, and many others who touched hundreds of lives. I realized that my work could reach many thousands of people, not just the few that graced my door.

On this day however, I felt sad and alone. There were very few books if any that talked about what I was doing. I knew of no one else that was clearing the energy field like I was. The Americans that said they had come to New Zealand to find me and awaken my knowledge of healing gave me their business card and told me to write to them with any questions I had. I had at least one-hundred questions in my first six months. I posted my letter and waited eagerly for a reply. Nothing came. I then decided to phone the number on the card. An elderly woman in America answered the phone and verified the number I had called. No, she had never heard of Robert and Helena and she had had the same phone number for the last thirty years!

I was both sad and mad. I felt very alone with no mentor or supervisor to give me guidance, surrounded by a sea of emotional releases and the associated "miracles" that followed.

"Where is everyone else?"

Suddenly there was an intense pressure on the top of my head. This had happened twice before. It pre-empted going into a deep trance. It was the depth of trance you may achieve after a lengthy meditation of conscious relaxation except it happened within a few moments and it was as if I had no control over it.

"No, no! I can't go that deep now," I insisted.

I was having a half-hour break between sessions and needed to head back to my work room.

"My client will arrive and wonder where I am."

I should have known better than to try and control it. It was futile. The pressure on my head grew stronger as if pushing me under, and suddenly I was in a world of effortless ease as everything in my body let go. What body? Floating. Bright swirling colors.

And then I heard her. A woman's voice, as clear as day spoke softly in my left ear, "Look in the eyes of the children. They are coming."

As swiftly as I had descended into trance, I was back, sitting on the grassy bank. I opened my eyes and there, staring right at me through a small wire fence four feet away, was a young boy about three years old with piercing blue eyes. It was as if he looked into me and right through me and I could look right through him. There were no guards or barriers between us. I had just received direct spiritual guidance and was so overwhelmed by this show of support that I burst into tears. The blue eyes just continued to look at me. The child totally accepted my tears as normal and acceptable. After a while, he just smiled, raised his tiny hand, opening and closing it to wave goodbye, turned, and ran to play with the other children. My eyes followed him and I realized that I was right beside a daycare facility. The children had come outside for their lunch break while I was in meditation.

I will never forget the complete openness of that child. That was twenty-seven years ago. It was 1987 and the higher frequency beings were beginning to arrive. That boy will be a thirty-year-old man today (2014) and I wonder what he is doing with his life.

Support through divine guidance from the spirit world exists and is available to all of us. We however must become the higher frequency of fourth- and fifth-dimensional energy to be able to experience that support—to hear them (clairaudience), to see them (clairvoyance), to feel or intuit them (clairsentience). We receive guidance from our own all-wise self when in a state of clear consciousness. There are also many advanced beings without bodies that exist in the higher realms that are ready and willing to assist us.

I had always known that spirits worked with me. I felt them like a cool breeze and a tingling down the back of my neck when they arrived. I did not always know if they were healing guides of mine or visitors for the client I was working with. It was about this time that three different clients at three different times saw and described the same Chinese man with a long black plait standing behind me, his arms extended with his radiant hands working through mine. Guidance repeated the message three times. After the third time, I chose to accept the old Chinese man's *support*. I learned that I would only receive support if I asked for it, so I began to acknowledge and appreciate his presence with some miraculous results.

After the experience of hearing the woman's voice, I never again questioned the amount of *support* that was available to me. I also understood more about how our work, when we assist others, reaches far and wide like a giant ripple effect that passes from person to person across the globe.

⁓ 12 ⁓

Up the Frequency!: 27 Years Old

Teaching: Ask and You Shall Receive

I was finished with work for the day. Okay, my turn. I lay down on my healing table and tucked a pillow under my knees to alleviate any pressure on my lower back. I would spend some time completely relaxing my body and then use my mind to run different color frequencies to open all the energy circuits. My body twitched and jerked as various realignments occurred. I sounded various harmonic notes until I felt the familiar tingling of higher-frequency energy in motion. The body was falling, falling, until it was no more and I floated in the alert bliss of no body.

'I wonder how much energy I can bring through this body?' I wondered.

In spirit I am a much finer frequency than this dense physical mass. I want to feel it.

"I really wanna see you Lord . . . it takes so long my Lord . . . Hallelujah." (George Harrison)

My breathing is steady and even. I am vaguely aware of my body in deep trance. I really want to feel my higher-frequency God self. It feels like a deep longing, almost like the ache of feeling homesick.

"I want my higher frequency in my body now. Up the frequency! So be it!" I demand through thought.

I focus with all my intention.

"Up the frequency!" I demand again.

My body begins to vibrate from head to foot. This was good. Something was happening. I was feeling a real hum through my body. This continued and was constant over the next hour. I refused to give up. I had nothing but time and I was not leaving this space until I knew how much energy could come through my body. "More! Up the frequency!"

Suddenly it felt as if the top of my head had split open with a three-inch gouge deep into my brain that was filled with white light. It flashed down through my face and neck in a split second and continued into my chest area and then shot off to the left, unable to enter my lower body. My back arched up off the table as I gasped in shock. The white light was so bright that I felt completely blinded for some time. I opened my eyes and could not see. For a while I thought I had done some permanent damage to my eyes.

"That'll learn ya. You've gone and blinded yourself with the light!" I scolded.

Slowly my body regained full sensation and my vision returned.

"Did that really just happen?" I asked myself.

"Wow! I was not expecting that."

It was as if some great "God being" got tired of my incessant demands "Up the frequency . . . up the frequency . . . ra . . . ra . . . ra."

"Oh, give her a taste of what she wants. Here!" he tosses a great shaft of light in my direction. "There. That should shut you up! Ask and you shall receive!"

Through absolute determination and focus I had experienced a small taste of a much higher frequency than what I was familiar with on planet Earth, or more accurately what I was presently capable of bringing through physical form. I had managed to give myself a real fright. Why was I afraid? My skull splitting open, the thought that I was permanently blind, and a great beam of light exploding into my chest just to name a few.

I knew immediately that my body could not house such a high frequency.

I spent all my days in my healing clinic clearing people's energy fields, especially the lower earth centers to enable the upper spiritual centers and heart center to get bigger. The more energy that could get through, the more likely the person had the experience of "waking up." They would realize that they were greater than their small world of constant toil, filled with petty emotions and grievances, and were more likely to see the bigger picture with the understanding that they had forgotten they were great beings that were capable of so much more. The key was the ability to *love*. Love and the higher frequency were one and the same. As the heart expanded, it was the "bridge" for energy to pass into the dense matter of the three-dimensional body. This in turn raised the frequency of energy available to the body on a cellular level. As the body became lighter, the upper centers could channel more energy and the being would feel more love and so on. Just like a river, if more water feeds into it, it will move faster. The faster the frequency, the more we step out of the density of third-dimensional matter and experience fourth-, fifth-, and sixth-dimensional energy with all the positive and loving thoughts that came with that.

I was tired of the sad stories, the accumulated Earthbound pain, and just wanted to bathe in the light for a while.

To fully earth the higher frequency that burst through my crown center that day, my heart needed to be bigger and more pure to be the bridge for that energy to live in my body. I learned that I may not be ready to radiate in my light body, but that light frequency was who I really was. We were all great beings of a *higher frequency*.

⌐ 13 ⌐

Seeing Through the Veil:
28 Years Old

Teaching: Spirits

It was late. About 11 p.m.

"I should go to bed. Another big day tomorrow."

I was running my Wellington clinic and my days started early and ended late as I fit all my clients in before flying home. Wellingtonians had asked me some time ago if they could fly me down and house me rather than all of them having the expense of traveling north. It certainly made sense.

I had the house to myself for four days while the owner was away and was just finishing up a few notes at the dining room table after a late dinner. Directly opposite me was a glass ranch slider door that led to a small deck. I had not bothered to pull the curtains as it faced the privacy of a bush reserve and the stars were pleasant.

I packed up my paperwork and stretched as I noted my reflection in the glass door. In the next few minutes, I stared incredulously as my face suddenly changed to that of an older woman wearing an old-fashioned stylish hat. She smiled at me and waved. I shook my head and again saw my reflection.

"It is late and you are overdoing the work because now you are seeing things!" I scolded myself.

My reflection changed again. This time it was a man in a military uniform. He removed his hat and bowed his head in acknowledgement to me.

"What the . . . ?"

His face changed to that of a young sailor with a cheeky grin.

"I am not imagining this. These people are saying hello to me." I shook my head violently in case my vision was playing tricks on me. I had not consumed any alcohol and I was not taking any prescription medication.

A middle-aged woman in a bonnet was next. She blew me a kiss. I decided to say hello, and in that moment of acknowledgement the faces came faster and faster until I could hardly keep up with them. Women, men, teenagers, and juveniles. They all wanted to say hello, tipping their hats and waving.

The kaleidoscope of faces was over as fast as it had begun. I sat stunned, looking at my own dark reflection in the glass door. Were they all different spirits just saying hello or perhaps connected to my clients and thanking me for my work?

Could they be my past lives as they all felt familiar?

All I know is that it was as real as turning on a TV screen. It only ever happened the one time, and no matter how many glass doors I gaze into, it hasn't happened since.

I understand now, that after an intensive day of work where I had worked with spirit for at least ten hours, I was in an open state of being and could *see through the veil*. The veil was like a transparent silk where spirits resided just on the other side. As I raised the frequency of my energy through my practice of healing, I was able to see what is always there.

I wondered what it was like for them, looking at us; like one of those underwater worlds, looking through thick glass panels. No wonder they seemed so thrilled when I waved back in acknowledgement and more and more faces became present. Imagine if the underwater stingray came up to the glass and winked at you.

"Look mum, he can see me! He said hello!"

There would be plenty more people rushing to see the communicating sea creature.

There are many beings that are not incarnate in physical form. Many would like a body, but cannot be allocated one at this time, and many spirits without bodies are taking a great interest in Earth and wish to visit our third dimension. No other planet has stooped to the density of the "dark ages" as Earth did and successfully risen again to the higher frequency of love and light. All eyes are on Earth to observe her re-awakening. It is a wonderful time to be here with personal spiritual development assured if you are present on Earth at this time. No wonder there are queues of beings trying to get here, and if you do not fully appreciate your opportunity to become a more loving, conscious being, there are beings that will happily "cadge a ride." If you spend time away from your physical body through unconscious pursuits like drug and alcohol abuse, another being will literally attach itself to you and feed off your energy field.

You may feel, well, not quite yourself. ☺

Long-term attachments from troubled souls can be responsible for the disease process, and general lethargy through to severe mental illness.

People can choose to believe, or not, spiritual attachments, haunted houses, or spirits in general that are having trouble "crossing over" after death. I have never been a follower or a blind believer, preferring to have my own experiences of such things.

I was thirty-eight years old and had agreed to help out one day a week on the ward for Acute Mental Health. I was allocated care of a young eighteen-year-old girl. As I was looking at her art folder, I noticed numerous self portraits, each one of them depicting the same dark shadow over the left side of her head.

"What does the shadow mean?" I queried.

"That is the man who tells me to cut myself. He says I have to, because I am evil," she said with sadness. Her arms were heavily bandaged from the last episode slashing at her arms that pre-empted her recent admission.

I had been working with clearing "spiritual clutter" for fifteen years and could not help myself from at least trying to assist this girl when she had her whole life ahead of her.

"Would you like to do some relaxation exercises?" I asked her.

"Yes," she said, quite matter of factly.

"Okay, lie down on your bed."

I covered her with a blanket and instructed her to close her eyes. As my hand ran around her head I leapt with fright, not expecting such a quick response. It is a feeling like being bitten or stung, enough to quickly retract my hand. I set about clearing the girl's possession by calling on my spiritual support and surrounding the hate-filled being with such a high frequency of love that it would have to release. A short time into this procedure there was a knock on the door and there stood the girl's mother.

"Hello," I smiled. "We are just doing some relaxation. I will be finished in a few minutes."

"How wonderful!" the mother exclaimed. "You continue. I can come back tomorrow."

"No please, just wait a few minutes. I won't be long," I encouraged.

"Alright. I will go the kitchen and make us both a hot chocolate."

She turned and was gone. I then broke all my own rules. I did not follow protocol. I rushed the healing and left things incomplete. I turned to leave the room.

"Your mum will be back soon."

I got as far as the door and the whole room began to spin. I grabbed the door handle to steady myself. My vision became blurred and I felt nauseous. I knew exactly what had happened and chastised myself for tackling such difficult work so casually and putting the needs of the girl's mother before my own safety.

I got as far as the nursing station and called, "Taking the early dinner."

"Okay, fine. See you later," the nurse in charge called back from within the office.

My head was pounding. I could not believe it was happening, nor my stupidity. I intuitively went straight to the big trees in the small park close to the ward all the while calling the beings of light, the archangels, and Jesus to assist this troubled being that had attached to me back to the spirit world where he could receive healing and guidance. I was familiar with aggressive beings determined not to leave and this was one of them.

I sat at the base of the largest, strongest tree and calmed myself, breathing in its mighty essence and quietly said my prayers for the lost soul. As my body relaxed and I felt the familiar peace come over me, the fight around my head seemed to increase. I had no vision at all as everything before me was blurred. I was so amazed to be experiencing what had been troubling the girl first-hand that my fascination overrode my fear. My spiritual faith in my guidance and assistance was so strong that at no time did I fear for my long-term safety. The young girl's attachment had been severe enough for her to self harm and I had approached it much too casually. I remained very calm in just the way I had been trained, gently speaking with the being in a loving way, yet firmly. There was no way he could stay!

I must have remained like this in prayer for at least fifteen minutes before I felt the moment the pressure left from my crown center. It was like my head was suddenly filled with cotton wool and a glorious tingling cascaded down my arms and legs. I opened my eyes and everything was clear with radiant color. I felt immense gratitude for the spiritual assistance I had received and great relief that my ordeal was over.

I stayed under the tree for some time contemplating what I had experienced. I had never felt the power of a very negative attachment before and had a whole new respect for *spirits* present on the Earth without bodies.

There are also cases of bodies without spirit. A teacher of mine said, "You only need 1 percent of the great being that you are to get up and brush your teeth."

This is enough spiritual attachment to the body for the vital functions to continue, including the autonomic nervous system responsible for heart rate, digestion, respiratory rate, salivation, perspiration, breathing, and swallowing.

There was another case on the same ward whereby there was a young woman about nineteen years old who had disassociated from her body after giving birth. The medical term is post-partum catatonia. She had been admitted on Monday, and by the time I joined the ward on Sunday she had not moved, spoken, or consumed any-thing by mouth for one week. She had a catheter inserted for urine, an intravenous drip for Dextrose Saline and had not moved her bowels since her admission. The ward had set up her bed in the day room so that there was room for her large extended Maori whanau to care for her.

After reading the case notes, I asked permission of the elders present if I could give their mokopuna natural spiritual healing. They said that they would be open to trying anything.

On previous shifts where I thought my work appro-priate I had either worked on patients behind the closed door of their room or taken them down to the rec room with pillows and blankets and laid them down on the table tennis table! This was quite different. I had a rather large audience.

I said my karakia (prayer) and went about my work to find where the spirit had gone. My guess was that the trauma and pain of the birth had triggered the memory of previous trauma and pain, in this life or another, and it was severe enough for the spirit to refuse to return.

The young woman's energy was at least twelve feet away. It took some time to "bridge" her energy closer to her body and to begin to feel some energy flow to the tissues and organs. After about an hour I left her while she was still unconscious. As I was leaving my shift at 11 p.m., the family excitedly reported that her bowels had moved and she was moving her left hand. When I rang to see how she was progressing the following morning she had her eyes open, had swallowed water and jelly, and had shuffled about eight feet to use the toilet.

The kuia (grandmother) wrote to the hospital board to outline what had occurred for her moko and to state that this was the healing that was needed for the Te Arawa people. The tribe had originally gifted the land that the hospital was built on, on the understanding that Te Arawa could always access hospital services. Sadly, the kuia did not receive a reply nor did the hospital investigate this case further.

It was clear to me that *spirits* were alive and well when not incarnate in a body and they were also capable of sitting well outside of the body. This explained some cases of cot death where the spirit never fully arrived to "take up" the body or decided in the first few months to return to the spirit world. The being was not dead, only the vehicle for their journey on Earth that required a spiritual connection with Source to survive.

❧ 14 ❧

Which Way is Up?: 30 Years Old

Teaching: Trust

Spinning, spinning, what seems like endless rolling through the water. The side of my face hurts where it hit the surface at 40 mph and I realize as my body stops the spinning continues inside my head. I can't see. Dizzy, spinning, dizzy in the blackness and I feel myself leaving, unconscious.

From somewhere in my body an alert signal is triggered. Within seconds I jolt back into body and understand that the pitch blackness is the deep, deep water of the lake. I cannot breathe! I am familiar with the feeling of being winded from my days on the hockey field. Every ounce of breath has been squeezed out of my body after the hard impact of my flying body hitting the glassy surface of the water. I see it coming. My body traveling like a torpedo through the air. There is nothing I can do to stop the inevitable impact.

Glorious summer days at Lake Rotoiti. I had spent the morning towing my wee nieces behind my new boat on the inflatable "biscuit" that I had bought especially for their holiday. They looked so cute in their little orange life jackets. The seven-year-old was not at all sure so the boat purred very slowly within the curve of the bay. In no time, there was much squealing and calls to go fast as I turned and crossed the wake of the boat. Bump, bump, bump, they held on tight over the waves.

Having dropped the babies off for their lunch, I leapt onto the inflatable and shouted to my brother-in-law, "You drive!"

"You betcha!" he smiled gleefully.

Ron had been dying to get behind the wheel and he quickly revved the outboard motor, towing me outside the 5 km swim zone. He soon guns the engine and I am flying along the surface of the water, bouncing and bumping over the small waves. He is traveling too fast and I can only just hold on. White knuckled, I am unable to release one of my hands to signal him to slow down for fear of falling. My first mistake is that I have no lookout scout on board the boat to read my discomfort and most of the time Ron's back is turned watching where he is going. I call as loud as I can, but as he looks over his shoulder to me he mistakes this for laughter and with a grin he accelerates further. I am gripping the side handles with all my might. I do not want to come off and hit the water at this speed and am cursing my stupidity for not putting on a life jacket. The muscles of my forearms are burning.

"Mate. . . . Slow down!" I have mixed emotions ranging from genuine fear to outrage for Ron's 'gung-ho' foolishness.

"No, no, please don't turn!"

Any "boatie" knows that when turning, you need to slow down as the person you are towing shoots out to the opposite side of the boat and picks up considerable speed. Only halfway into the turn the inflatable biscuit is no

Close to Death, Closer to God

longer governed by the laws of gravity and is airborne. My hands are yanked free from their hold and I am soaring through the air.

Impact with the lake is hard, really hard, and I tumble and tumble like a rag doll in the darkness. It seems to take forever to stop tumbling through the water.

The propensity for panic is huge. I desperately want to hold my breath, but there is no breath to hold. The intense black engulfs me as I realize I am a long way from the surface. The fear locks my stomach like a vice, and I am totally disoriented.

I have no idea which way is up.

The desire to swim, to get out of the cold blackness is overwhelming. Air! Air! I have to have air!

"Relax until you float. You will know which way to swim."

The thought is simply there. Where did it come from? Divine wisdom from within? Divine guidance? All I know is that with no air in my lungs and every reason to panic, this is what I have to do. Against every instinct to fight for control, I consciously let every muscle in my body go. There is a sweet feeling of falling and in that moment all struggle ceases. I am the lake and the lake is me. It feels easy like floating in a trance. I could be dying now.

In salt water, the body is very buoyant and floats easily. In the dense fresh water of the lake it seems to take an eternity for me to get any sense of floating. My lungs are on fire, threatening to give in and let the water pour in to cool the burning ache inside me.

I begin to feel the slight upward movement of my body. Up! I know which way is UP!

I claw for the surface like one possessed; possessed with the intention of living. After what seems a long time, I begin to see a glimmer of light above me. I feel a strange blotchy feeling in my head and I know I am close to losing consciousness. The light is coming and going from my vision. It is still so far away.

I break the surface with a gasp for air that sends a sweet wind to expand my ribs. The glare of the sunlight is blinding having escaped my dark coffin. My vision is blurred and my head is pounding. Eventually I see the hull of the boat come along side me.

"Gees, I couldn't see you anywhere. You gave me a bit of a fright!" Ron exclaimed.

All I could manage was, "You idiot."

There was a new rule on the boat after that day. No one went without a life jacket, there always had to be a lookout scout, and only sensible drivers need apply.

Trust was the lesson of the day. I had to trust the divine guidance that came through me telling me to relax when every cell in my body wanted to panic, kick, and fight. Without those few seconds of complete relaxation I would not have known which way to swim and would have died in the deep inky water of the lake.

In extreme circumstances where absolute *trust* is required, divine wisdom resides.

This all knowing is within each of us. When it was as important as life or death, I could tap into divine wisdom. I did not have to seek wisdom or grow old to become wise, for wisdom already existed—the God force itself residing in me.

If wisdom was God and the life force that is God is in all things, then the all knowing was everywhere, in all matter. When I surrendered my body to *trust* the wisdom that with relaxation, my body would float, I was no longer in the conflict of fear and panic.

My mind directs every event. When confronted with extreme emotional reaction, I could practice the discipline set by my mind and I was capable in a split second of moving from chaos to serene relaxation! I could conquer my emotions by disciplining my mind and instead tapped into divine wisdom. To be in my divine wisdom was to be in present time in the presence of the still, calm energy that is God.

Why had I not discovered how quickly I could do this before? The answer is simple really. Because I did not need to or did not want to. Nothing was rushing me to move out of my emotional state; in fact I may even be enjoying it. I could spend some time punishing you just a little longer, judging or gossiping a little longer. I may want to hang on to the notion that I am right for a little longer. If my life did not depend upon it, there was no hurry to move past my arrogance, the stroking of my ego, or whatever other over indulgences I wanted to wallow in. I could be lazy, self-serving, and a mere fraction of the great being that I am and fit right in with the majority.

And all this time, wisdom was there for the taking. I could conquer all conflict emotionally and mentally by holding my focus completely in this moment where there was no distraction, meaningless thoughts, or judgments. If I just held my focus on the task at hand with a passion like my life depended on it, I could *trust* in my divine wisdom—the presence of God. This opened up my world to infinite possibility. It took *trusting* my wise guidance within to be able to step out of my own way. It was only a destructive thought away or a flicker of doubt that stopped manifestation in its tracks. To *trust* meant letting go and not trying to control the situation. In everyday life, we simply don't want to. It is a lot easier not to practice conscious discipline and throw emotional panic every which way. I had to conquer control over my emotions to survive that day. I imagined taking that skill into everyday stressful situations, to be able to master that level of discipline even when confronted with another's chaos. I enjoyed the fantasy of becoming the observer in the face of personal attack, to master having no reaction.

The very next day while driving through a new shopping mall road layout, I received my first test. I went to turn into a parking area that I had used previously. I saw that it had been changed and was now a curb. What had been an entrance was now blocked. This meant that I had to stop, reverse, and continue to travel around the roundabout. Thankfully, there was no one behind me for me to inconvenience.

From the far side of the roundabout a young woman with her window down, took it upon herself to scream at the top of her lungs, "Get a f . . . king driver's license!!"

In years past, I would have had an instant reaction of indignation.

"I haven't bothered her at all. It is none of her business."

I may have even shouted back, if I mustered enough self-righteous rage.

Instead, in mere seconds, I took in the pained look on her face, the beat-up car, and three crying young children standing on the back seat, not strapped in. In one glance her life spelt frustration and hardship. As I traveled the roundabout, I had to drive right past her. I lowered my window and slowed. Her face scowled, ready for the fight and all I could feel was compassion.

"Are you having a rough day?" I inquired without a hint of patronage. She could feel my genuine caring for her and her mouth literally fell open with shock as all rage left her face. I had to keep moving as there was traffic behind me.

I experienced a great lesson that day. I could *trust* my ability to tap into my wise loving self even when being abused emotionally.

With this *trust* I felt an unstoppable power within.

≈ 15 ≈

One Family: 31 Years Old

Teaching: Love

A rriving in the little float plane was exciting. The Sounds were so beautiful. A mass of secluded inlets and what looked like islands as the landmass sprawled north, holding its tentative grip on the South Island of New Zealand. Many of the remote, picturesque bays were only accessible by boat, and Endeavour Sound was one of them. My friend Pat peered out the window of the little Cessna float plane as we prepared to land.

"I wonder which cottage we are staying in," she squealed with delight.

I smiled at Pat's standard poodle strapped in to her own seat, panting eagerly as she spotted land. This did more to humanize her than her fluffy pigtails and all of her trendy restaurant visits put together.

Our pilot knew all the properties within the bay and landed outside the appropriate rickety jetty. The cottage had been inherited by one of my clients from his late grandfather.

"Feel free to use it any time you like, Meryl. It's nothing flash, and be careful: the dinghy leaks, but just bail it out now and again."

Nothing flash was a bit of an understatement. It was an ancient, untouched bach (or crib as they call them in the South) that belonged to the charm of yesteryear until you saw the rat poo everywhere. I can do simple and I can do old, but I cannot abide dirty or vermin. We would not see the float plane again for a week, so we figured we had best make the most of it. The first thing we set about doing was to completely clean the kitchen and living room. We brought the beds out from the bedroom, aired them in the sun, and set up our sleeping camp in the living room, closing off all other rooms with plenty of rat bait and towels stuffed under the doors.

It was early Spring and still chilly in this part of the world after about 2 p.m. The only form of heating and cooking was the old wood coal range. I had never operated one before, but figured if we didn't want to freeze or starve, I had better learn fast. There was always the back up of Endeavour Sounds Lodge, a twenty-minute walk away through the bush, but I did not fancy the return trek in the dark and freezing cold. There was plenty of dry wood, and I soon worked out how to open all vents and then direct the flame to the oven compartment. I have never been so proud of a roast chicken with vegetables in all my life. That wee cooker also heated all the hot water and there was a kerosene lamp and ample candles to light at night. In other words, without a box of matches you were completely "poked" on all fronts. I had a brief thought for my distant ancestors and felt grateful that I did not have to find the right sticks to rub together.

"He never told me there would be no power!" I exclaimed.

Pat rolled her eyes. I don't think she knew what had hit her having always enjoyed life with a "silver spoon." She was stuck in the middle of nowhere, albeit a very beautiful nowhere, with only a fire as a lifeline to warmth, hot food, and showering. The poodle and I loved it! There was something incredibly earthy about no frills and basic survival, and let's face it, we didn't have to grow our own food or milk the goat.

That first night we heard the scurry of rats on the wooden floors in the neighboring rooms. The smell of the dog and the rat bait kept them away from the living room. By the third night all signs of them were gone.

The fire crackled and flickered in the coal range, the room dimly lit by candlelight, and I felt a deep peace in my simple world away from the demands of home.

"I'm going to try a bit of fishing tomorrow," I stated optimistically. "I will see what gear is out the back. They say there is plenty of blue cod."

"You're not getting me in that leaky dinghy," Pat laughed.

She had cheered up immensely after a full tummy, a glass of wine, and a cigi on the front deck as a glorious sunset flooded the bay with pinks and orange. It was way too magical to feel unhappy for long.

"Yep, a good read of my book will do me." She stretched and yawned, not far from bed.

I rose with the sun and cranked up the coal range. It was cold and a wonderful mist hung over the mirrored water like the out breath of God steaming up the landscape. I sat on the old front veranda wrapped in a woolen jersey with a mug of hot coffee. It was so beautiful! Poodle mania was happening up in the bush with the sudden scent of a rabbit.

"The old man must have loved his time here," I pondered and gave him silent thanks.

There was petrol in the tank and some hand lines. I pinched a piece of meat off the steak thawing for dinner and pushed the two-wheeled cradle with the dinghy down to the water's edge. The motor roared with a couple of pulls. Oars on board, a life jacket, and a cut out plastic Janola bottle tied to the boat with a string for a bail. I didn't go far out into the bay before hooking a piece of meat and unwinding some line into the deep blue, green water. What looked like a homemade sinker slowly took my hook to the bottom. I said a silent karakia and asked for fish to grace our table. Within moments I had hooked my first cod and pulled it into the boat. I killed it swiftly with the point of my knife through its brain and thanked it for the gift of its life. I lowered the same piece of meat back into the sea and to my astonishment it was only moments before landing the next cod. I watched as the sea water oozed through a missing rivet hole on the floor of the boat, which required stopping to bail every ten minutes or so.

Whoa! Third cod in the boat. This continued with the same piece of meat until I had caught eight fish. They were small, about twelve inches long, but would make a delicious lunch. I was about to kick start my motor and head for the bach when I heard a crashing sound coming from somewhere just out of the bay. I listened with interest as the sound continued. It sounded like trees being felled and falling into the water, but there was no sound of chainsaws.

"What is that crashing noise?"

The motor roars to life as my inquisitiveness gets the better of me. Instead of heading for shore, I decide to head out around the small headland to see what all the kerfuffle is about. As I round the rocky promontory, there before me are huge dolphins slamming their tails down on the water. I can barely believe my eyes at the wonderful spectacle before me. As I slow to a crawl, I notice the shadows swimming under my dinghy. There are mothers with the most adorable babies swimming on either side of me. I am right in the middle of a massive pod. I begin to talk animatedly to them and the mothers lift their heads from the water with cheeky grins and called in response.

"Oh my goodness. They are talking to me!" I can barely describe my excitement. This is how you would feel to meet a family member that you dearly loved after not seeing them for a very long time. The babies! I just wanted to cuddle the babies!

The big males were slapping the water to bring the young ones into the center as they protectively flanked the outside of the pod, and they began to move as one, out to sea. I found myself naturally increasing my speed to move with them. This seemed to excite the mothers and babies even more as they dived under my boat and the little ones danced up to the surface. I yearned to catch a glance of their adorable faces and suddenly realized I was laughing, really laughing, and I could not stop. The wind pushed back my hair, the cod bounced about on the floor of the boat, and it was as if I had died and gone to heaven! I was truly experiencing heaven on Earth.

With a huge whoosh, the male dolphins leapt into the air either side of me, first two, then four, then six. As their huge bodies arched to dive, the spray of the water was a mass of rainbows glinting in the sun. I had never felt such exhilaration in all my life. I was whooping and yelling with the tears of my laughter blurring my sight. My boat was at full speed now and I was only just keeping up. I lost all sense of time. It could have been five minutes or half an hour. I had no idea. All I knew was happiness. I had never felt such raw unguarded joy. I laughed and laughed and laughed.

I glanced toward my feet and saw the cod floating. The water was just above my ankles. Reality returned like a full stop. I had no idea how much fuel I had left, but I was quite a long way off shore and knew that I must return. With huge regret I slowed my boat as I said my heartfelt goodbye and to my amazement the pod slowed with me. I was family and they would not leave me behind. Two of the females stopped still as my boat came to an idle, their snub noses high in the air as they balanced with their tails and squeaked the most adorable sounds. I could see the dark wetness of their eyes looking directly at me and my heart exploded in a rush of the most pure feeling of *love* that I have ever experienced.

The only thing that came close to this was when a baby held your gaze and smiled. Even then, you know that life may hurt them and twist their innocence into an adult who is not loving. Not so with this family of mammals. It would not matter how badly we treated them; they may run and hide, but we could never deplete the pure *love* that was their essence. I knew in that moment, as I felt my heart expanding, that they were present on this Earth as examples of purity and joy for me to aspire to. They were my gurus (teachers).

"I am so sorry I have to go. I do not want to leave you," I cried with tears of both sadness and joy. "I love you. I love you," I called, as my family continued out to sea.

I look down at the water in my boat that is now slopping from side to side and bail my dinghy before returning to the safety of the bay.

For the rest of that day I could feel an extra vibration in my body as if everything had stepped up a notch. The images in my mind and the feeling in my heart will stay with me always. I had experienced that in my true essence I was absolute, uncontainable *Love*.

I have always been respectful of the small creatures, intuitively knowing that all life is sacred and that we are one. I have no more right to kill the small spider than someone has the right to kill me. I gingerly coax it into a small container, fighting my fear of eight-legged furry things, and set it free outside in the undergrowth. The same respect for life has me freeing small mice and birds from the mouths of my feline companions or braving horrendous storms to bring baby lambs into the shed before they die of cold. I will not kill for food without exercising the utmost compassion and gratitude.

"Thou shalt not kill." (Exodus 20:13)

As we rise in frequency, there will come a time when as humans we no longer kill animals to eat. Our bodies survive very well on plants, some grains, legumes, and nuts, which is how we lived a very long time ago.

One year my elderly ewe that always gave me triplets was heavily pregnant and due to drop any day. I watched her as she could not keep her balance on a steep hillside and was about to topple over, resulting in a nasty fall and the possible loss of her lambs. She slowly lost her balance and without thinking I threw myself under her body as she fell. My body took the full brunt of the fall as we slipped together down the hill. It must have been quite a sight; my arms wrapped around this heavy sheep, both of us on our backs with her huge pink udder exposed, crashing down the hill. I tore the ligaments across the top of my buttocks that day and was laid up on the couch for a week. She had three beautiful babies and was allowed to retire the following year. She remained the matriarch of the flock until she died. I could open all the gates, stand at one end of my thirty acres and call her, "Sheep, sheep sheeeep."

She always knew this meant fresh grass and quickly taught the rest of the flock to come running. I could not see them past the deep valleys, but would hear the low thunder of many hooves. I could move the sheep anywhere on the farm, including the yards for drenching and docking, singlehandedly without a farm dog.

I experience a true love for the land and genuine happiness when connecting with the animals and nature; the smell of the earth and the crisp clean air. I totally understand why once a farmer, always a farmer. If raised on the land, it would call to you and you would yearn for wide-open spaces and the smell of a wood fire.

My experience with the dolphins brought a whole new understanding of how I was connected to all things. When I was immersed in the energy of those wild, carefree mammals, I felt their sheer, untamed joy, which was also me. When there was no clutter in my mind, no negative thoughts, just the freedom of being, there was *only love*. I have no other memory in my lifetime of such laughter that poured through me like the endless flow of a mighty river.

The experience in the old cottage added to this lesson. I could have complained at the filth, the rodents, no power, the leaky boat, or spending money on airfares traveling to a place I did not initially want to stay, but the overwhelming beauty of nature and my experience of *love* had me purring with contentment.

I looked at everything differently after that day in the boat. I walked with a softer tread in the bush so as not to disturb the fernery. I said extra prayers for the dying rats and felt a deep respect for the fish, which gave me food. The God-Force was in them as it was in me. As physical matter, we were one and the same. As a human being, I have been given dominion over the animals, creatures, and plants. With this comes the responsibility of caring for them, sustaining them, and using them for sustenance with consciousness.

All living matter is capable of emotion. A man named Anthony Lawrence, dedicated his life to the rescue and rehabilitation of elephants. When he died aged sixty-two years, two matriarch elephants led a herd twelve miles to his home. They were joined by a second herd from another area entirely. A total of thirty-one elephants stayed outside his home for two days and two nights. Something in the Universe is greater than human intelligence. The matriarch elephants not only new the time of death of a man they considered one of their extended family or a friend whose kindness they remembered, but they knew exactly where he was. They had an energetic connection with him because he had shown them love.

There are many stories of dogs who have done heroic things to save humans from death. Their loyalty is born out of *love*.

Dr. Masaru Emoto discovered that you could freeze different emotions in water. The water exposed to *love* has perfectly aligned crystals as opposed to the chaotic crystals of hate.

Peaceful, happy gardeners were said to have a green thumb as their plants responded to their loving frequency, and food tastes better when cooked with love.

I had experienced the energy frequency within the pod of dolphins. The males cared to protect their families. The females cared for their young, and when they slowed down as my boat dropped in speed, they cared for me. In the midst of that experience, I was not in my left brain of logical thought; the boat is leaking, the fuel may run out, or I am too far from land. For a brief time, I was totally immersed in the divine feminine of right brain. This is the energy that can heal and balance all the atrocities on our planet. People touch it when they write a poem or a piece of music, when they are immersed in the dance, at play, or gaze into the eyes of a child or loved one. In that moment there is no such thing as time. In divine present time with the balance of left and right brain where all joy resides, there is only our essence, which is *love*.

Love is the natural condition as created by the God-Force. All that is beautiful and perfect is *the law of love* and we were designed to live in this state of love, daily. This was true for an ancient civilization much older than we believe our planet to be, when we all lived in the higher vibrational state of Ascended Masters. As mankind gave more and more of his focus to his external world and away from his source, which *is love*, he steadily descended into chaos. Our world, instead of pure perfection, became one of duality: positive and negative, right and wrong, good and evil. This is symbolized in the Bible as partaking of the forbidden fruit. Once duality existed, the freedom of perfection was no more.

We now experience the constant chatter of thoughts and the subsequent cluttered emotion that follows. We choose to hold on to the thoughts, usually at the insistence of being right, or to indulge in our fears, and then our being is swamped with feelings of emotional pain, resentment, anger, and worry.

It took being in the presence of my mammalian family to discover the space within myself devoid of all "negative" emotion or thought that was pure, ecstatic joy. For a long time, I thought of the joy as belonging to the dolphins. They lived in a pure state of love and I yearned to be them, free in the wild with no worldly responsibility and no human emotional clutter around me. I awakened to the truth that what I had experienced *was me* and it was up to me to discipline my thoughts, feelings, and actions if I ever wanted such a pure experience of love again.

Whatever lacks love is not fully formed in substance, and there is nowhere in creation that it can survive for long. As chaos, it must return to substance to reform into perfection. This is a Universal Law.

This helps us to understand our disease processes and lack of longevity. Our bodies survived a great deal longer in ancient times as perfected substance because of our higher frequency of love. We currently, rapidly return to substance, most of us in less than one hundred years because of our chaotic destructive thoughts.

We all know of someone who was kind and non-judgmental that expressed love for others, especially children, animals, and nature, that lived to a ripe old age. It was their ability to *love* that kept their bodies from diseasing sooner.

Imagine a time when you have felt intense love, and then imagine this feeling without being distracted by irritation, frustration, anger, disappointment, fear, judgment, and other painful emotions. There are higher realms of consciousness both cosmically and individually that experience *love* as constant joy, freedom, and perfection. They are more real than life as we know it because they are forever expanding with no disintegration.

The more we strive for this, consciously choosing not to have such damaging thoughts, emotions, or speech, the more we experience blessings and joy in our true perfection.

Human appetites and desires from the outer self accumulate "misqualified energy" from thoughts and feelings that become habit. The appetites of former lives added to the habits of this life keep us enslaved to continuous embodiments of lack and suffering until we learn to obey the *law of love*.

Love alone is the right use of all life energy. The human experience of this is the desire to give our individual peace and harmony to the rest of creation.

It is only when we collectively experience enough *love* that we will return to the heaven on Earth we once knew.

One must first ask the question, "What is the reason for my misery?"

When we are willing to forgive and release cluttered emotion, enabling us to feel calm, peaceful, kindness, our heart center is activated and we can begin our journey back toward perfection. The great God flame lives within the heart and pours itself into substance as perfection.

Perfection manifested is *Love*.

Love is source.

Love is God.

❦ 16 ❧

"Waimarama": 34 Years Old

Teaching: The Void

What on earth have I done? It was three in the morning and I couldn't sleep.

I finished building Waimarama Healing and Education Centre. I moved away from my familiar community in the North to the Bay of Plenty, North Island, and sold valuable real estate assets to commit to my ambitious project. I closed my regular healing clinics in Northland, Auckland, and Sydney and only kept my Wellington clinic open, which I attended once a month. I had in effect doubled my debt and halved my income.

I had also placed myself in a remote environment where nobody knew where I was, which effectively stopped the daily parade of clients that would normally grace my door.

I had nothing but time, which initially felt like a great emptiness. Within the emptiness there would be waves of panic.

"My God, what have I done?"

Fear accompanies the unfamiliar, and an undisciplined mind can run headlong into the future, which is a haze of the unforeseen. There is nothing absolute, nothing certain. There cannot be, for the future has not yet happened.

The future is where all fear resides, and it controls us like an insidious sludge, holding us back from our potential as we play it safe in a world of so-called guarantees. These are called insurance, job promotion, and even marriage for some. Even if it means that you play out the same routine every day of your life, open the same shop door, or sit at the same desk, you do it because you have security. You are safe when you know exactly what you are doing for the day and how much take-home pay you will have in your pocket. It is a trap where you have stopped being creative, but you are hardly about to leave and throw it all away when you have worked years to achieve your position.

Routine, position, financial security. I had none of that anymore. It was all gone.

More significantly, I did not have the daily affirmation from satisfied clients that I was a successful healer. Without the daily feedback from my clients, the ground I walked on felt a little shaky. As the weeks went by, I was having trouble continuing to *identify as a healer*. This had been my identity for twenty years. So, who was I? I had been so busy *doing* that I had lost sight of *who I am*.

I realized that this is what people must feel like when they retire. They may have been at the top of their field for forty years and now they faced the nothingness. They could try filling the space with a mass of hobbies and community projects, but that only worked as a distraction from the fear of confronting that thought, 'Who am I?'

A *retired accountant* is hardly an identity. "Hello there, I am a non-accountant."

That is not far off from being a "non-human being." There are hundreds of recorded cases of people who do not make this transition without a sense of worthlessness and depression. It is our elderly men that have the highest suicide rate.

I remember the fear acutely after finally finishing the building of Waimarama in 1997. All of the contractors left and the silence was deafening as I faced the nothingness of non-action. I decided I was blessed to be in a position to conquer this lesson at the grand age of thirty-seven years, not when I was older, physically less active, or more vulnerable.

Something I was studying at the time said, "To allow change in your life, you must embrace the void."

If I could embrace *the void*, the hollow emptiness would slowly fill with the new. This was the journey to transition, and no matter how much I wanted safety or guarantees, they were not there. I had to embrace stillness and calm the mind by exercising trust in present time.

Every day I would sit on Waimarama's headland and practice just sitting in *the void*. At first everything in the mind screamed, "Do something! You could do this or that. . . . Go back to nursing. . . . Sell up! . . .You should be doing something!"

Then there were the opinions of others because what I was doing pushed all their buttons of fear and insecurity.

"What are you *doing*? Do you have a plan? You had such well-paid work. You could have made a lot of money in music you know. How could you just walk away? Oh it wouldn't suit me way out here. Why do you want to be out here on your own? If you scream, no one can hear you . . . blah blah blah."

Great! Now I am conquering my own fears and I've got yours bleating in my head too. The mind desperately wants to regain control, but it can only end up with the same result. Uncertainty, which begets anxiety, which begets fear, which begets the panic of not knowing. Worthless, useless, exhausting thoughts.

"Embrace the void."

I taught myself to breathe. To stop in each moment of beauty. To allow the nothingness. Slowly but surely the peace came. I did not find the peace, for peace need not be found. It already exists. *I am* peace, light, and love. This is how I began and it is only limited thought that clutters my energy with emotions of fear, believing that I am less than peace. Believing in limitation overwhelms my being, for I am not in control of my life. Life's circumstances are controlling me! This simply is not true.

I had a vision of a Healing Centre set high, away from the coast, and from the thoughts of my desire it had presented itself. I chose to sell the assets required to fully manifest the vision. I remember the day that I signed for the land, an unconditional cash sale. Later that night I could not sleep as I felt the fear of limited thought.

'What have I done? Where will my income come from? I hardly know anyone, stuck in the middle of nowhere! This is too hard. People are going to think I am crazy. I had a good life, friends, great income, and valuable investments.'

The next morning the phone rang early. It was the real estate agent. He apologized that he had made a mistake and shown me the wrong boundary for the property.

"This makes your contract null and void and you can step away from it if you wish," he explained.

It was as if the Higher Beings were saying, "If you don't want to do this, you don't have to."

I have always wondered if this particular real estate agent was prepared to forfeit his commission and had given me an out on purpose. Perhaps he could not sleep either, worrying about this young woman alone tackling a difficult development project, not for the fainthearted.

I could reverse everything and my life could go back to "normal." I was so flabbergasted by being given this opportunity that I did not know what to say. Eventually I asked for twenty-four hours before giving him an answer.

I returned to the property and spent a large part of the day there. I asked myself, 'How does it feel to lose this opportunity?'

I remembered the excitement that had coursed through my veins as I tramped every square inch of the land the day before.

What was that?

That was my I Am Presence totally in present time co-creating with the world in the realm of possibility before there was time for limited thought!

Any doubt after that was based in fear, just as the agent felt fearful for me. When I asked myself if creating a Healing Centre was what I wanted to do, the answer was a resounding "Yes" and yes, it was the ideal property with no neighbors, fifteen minutes from the airport, and exceptionally beautiful. I was aware that it would take everything I had achieved financially, but something much bigger than my safe, small ego self was driving me. It was the excitement of pure potential, which sets the spirit free to be the great unlimited being *I AM*. To not do this was to give in to the fearful voices in my head. And even though they made logical sense in many ways, I intuitively knew if I were to deny the dream, I was denying the self and all I was capable of. To allow that was to suffer a death, to give up on what I knew to be true, that we are great beings of light only limited by our own thoughts and fears.

"Embrace the void."

The calm found its way into each new day as I sat out on Waimarama's headland, which protruded out into the vast expanse of the lake with no other sign of humanity bar a few houses and a quiet road in the distance. It was like hanging on to the end of the world. Within the stillness was *the void*, the nothingness, empty of my life as I had known it, empty of security and affirmation of who I was. I had no job that I could identify with, no clients to confirm that I was a busy healer with numerous clinics. It was truly terrifying to surrender to *the void*.

Waimarama Healing and Education Centre would first be my teacher and my healer. I was the energy, all there is, that could manifest anything when stilling the mind of its fears.

"Wai Marama" (Water Moon). I had given the property this name in respect for the fact that it was part of the bigger Maori Trust block and was the only piece of land that had been subdivided off for a member of the Iwi (tribe). It had then found its way through a number of sales into nontribal ownership. The full moon would shine a light for miles on the water of Lake Rotoiti.

It was not until my partner of Ngapuhi descent joined me on the land that she spaced the syllables of the name:

"Wa i marama." Place of clarity/understanding or Time of enlightenment.

The void was slowly allowing the new to evolve.

There is a charming story that further describes this.

A young earnest student went in search of enlightenment. He studied every book and participated in every possible educational course in search of the answers. Eventually his search took him high into the Himalayas where, after many months, he found the simple shelter of a wise spiritual master.

"Master, oh master. I have searched for you all of my life! My greatest desire is to know enlightenment. I fall at your feet great Swami in the hope that you will be my guru."

He falls to his knees to kiss the sandals of his teacher.

"Up, up," says the wise man. "First, we must have tea."

They sit either side of a small wooden table and the teacher places a cup in front of each of them. The student, enthusiastic about receiving his first lesson, chats about all that he has studied and all that he has achieved to date. He is hoping to impress his teacher with his account of his many years of dedicated study.

The wise man silently picks up the teapot and begins to fill the student's cup. The student continues to talk as the cup fills and then overflows. The student does not pause to notice until the tea spills over the table and into his lap.

"Master, master! Stop, stop! The cup is already full. It can take no more!"

The teacher slowly puts down the teapot and speaks directly to the student.

"As it is with you. Your cup is full and overflowing."

He bowed deeply to honor the spirit of the student and departed, leaving the student to face the long journey back down the mountain.

To know *the void* was to empty my cup of much that had filled it in the past, which allowed the new to come.

❧ 17 ❧

Chanting: 38 Years Old

Teaching: Body Memory

The excruciating pain in my back is not going away. It is at the level of my heart and feels as if someone has pushed a dagger through my ribs, steadily twisting it. I am in the midst of a two-hour meditation with one thousand people. As my body relaxes further the pain increases more. Silent tears roll like rivers down my face.

I cannot take this pain any longer.

I am at an Ashram north of New York where I am booked for two weeks of intensive study and spiritual practice.

I was offered lucrative work on my way through Los Angeles after my healing work was recommended by a masseuse to the stars. She was so impressed by her increased energy flow that she told her entire client base. I am tested again with the distraction of notoriety if I would only change my plans to wait for various actors and movie personnel to return to Hollywood. Extending my business is not the focus of my trip, nor the passion in my heart, so I continue on my journey to San Francisco and catch my flight to New York as planned.

During the second day of meditation and chanting at the Ashram, I begin to experience the acute pain between my shoulder blades. I cannot shift it through yoga or various healing modalities available to me from other practitioners that are present at the Ashram. Eventually I beg for spiritual intervention.

"Please assist me with this pain. Whatever blockage is stored in my heart, I choose to release it! I am nothing less than my divine light of love and anything unlike that love must go! So be it!"

Not only is the pain immediately lifted, but I am lifted! Up, up, up, where the air is cool and thin in the highest mountains. I am in awe of the sheer size of the mountain range. "They" show me that I AM the mountains; I AM vast and span for miles.

"I can't possibly be this big!" I say to myself incredulously. I am in awe at what I am experiencing; totally free from my small Earth bound body, I am solid rock, stretching out with great arms that span the landscape.

After a while I realize how cold I am in my silent aloneness. A long way in the distance I can hear the group of people that I am residing with as they begin to chant, which marks the end of our meditation time.

"I want to be back with the people," I say quite clearly in my mind.

I begin to descend immediately. I can see the rooftop of the main meditation room and, in the next moment, I am back sitting heavily in my seat. There is no trace of the sharp unbearable pain between my shoulder blades.

Memory from another time can lock in the emotional field and manifest as pain and dis-ease in the physical body. It was not until I prayed for assistance and was taken to see the reality of the great being that I AM that I was able to release the density of emotion that was expressing itself through my body. I did not need to know all the details of what my pain was about as long as *the emotion attached to it released*. This released the *memory charge in my body* that was causing pain. Without this process, I would continue to create circumstances in my life to enable the release of those emotions to present them to my conscious mind for healing. If I did not find a way to release them, they had the power to stop my energy flow in its tracks, disease my body, and eventually be responsible for my death. This knowledge catapulted me into a passion for releasing such blockages in others. To constantly repeat emotional pain in the effort to heal was an unacceptable way to live, and to die prematurely from accidents or disease because our cells could not vibrate at the correct frequency was a failure of technology! With this knowledge also came the frustration of witnessing so much needless suffering.

As I joined in with the chanting, my eyes closed, I could see the approach of what appeared to be huge golden feathered arms. They were soon wrapped around my body and I felt a great peace like a deep sigh. Again I felt myself being lifted, weightless in a gentle rocking motion. I was tiny. Newly born. The intensity of the love I could feel was intoxicating.

"This is what the body needed. This is what was missing," I heard a soft reverent voice like a whisper.

After my birth, my poor mother would have been recovering from a general anesthetic and major abdominal surgery, which was required for caesarean section in 1960, and I would have been whisked away so that she could rest.

The memory of this experience cemented my belief that the baby once born should be placed skin on skin, on the mother's chest and covered with a blanket for warmth. The familiar sound of the mother's heartbeat assisted the transition from the warm amniotic sack to the stark reality of Earth. Thank goodness birthing procedures are more conscious of this these days. It was not long ago that every baby's first conscious moments involved physical pain as it was held by its ankles and spanked on the bottom to issue the first cry. It was then wrapped so tightly it must have felt like a straightjacket after the liquid bliss of the womb. Its first sounds were the distraught cries of other babies in the nursery often left alone and not held for long periods with the first suckling experience, distasteful sterile water.

Left with the mother, the baby would slowly gravitate to the nipple for the delicious taste of sweet colostrum; perfect temperature, perfect balance of essential vitamins and minerals, and perfectly satisfying. This first experience where all needs are met in a safe environment would have a huge effect later in life on the being's appetite for food and sex.

There was enough heartache ahead in the density of an Earthly existence without allowing the beginning to be as miserable as possible.

The "feathered angel" was showing me that the wound to my heart occurred in my first few breaths. This was a difficult block to heal and release, as I had no conscious memory of something happening that early in life. Even if I arrived in the body when it was already three years old, the painful memory had locked into the etheric field, which manifested as a blockage in the body. This was capable of twisting the spine with both hips and shoulders out of alignment by the age of five.

It was only because of the intense spiritual practice on the Ashram, that this *body memory* was able to surface for healing. During the pain of its extraction, I was taken on a journey to the mountains to see the bigger picture.

This I find is a common occurrence in my healing room as blockages are unearthed. People need time to process what is sometimes extreme emotion, and they separate away from the body, which allows the space to do this.

Body memory will show itself as an injury to the same part of the body that holds the memory and thus manifests as a weakness, or it may show up as an irrational fear or phobia that does not have its origin in this incarnation.

One of my clients many years ago had what appeared to be a completely irrational fear of flying. She would worry for days before a flight and by the time she was seated in the plane, her pulse would be elevated and she would begin to perspire. During one of her healing sessions she had a vivid recall of being a man in a World War I fighter plane. His last memory was nose diving at speed toward the water and certain death with flames around his cockpit. This memory had been stored in the etheric field and had returned with her in her current lifetime. Once the *body memory* was able to surface to consciousness, the body was able to release it as not relevant to present time. Even though this client would still prefer not to fly, the fear no longer has to bring itself to consciousness repetitively, which was incredibly debilitating.

⤜ 18 ⤝

Afternoon on the Lake: 41 Years Old

Teaching: Miracles

Janet had moved into a cute little cottage on the shores of Lake Rotoiti. The owner had said she could use the small twelve-foot aluminum dinghy. It had been a few months since I had sold my boat and I missed my regular trips to Manupirua Hot Springs, a picturesque spot on the edge of the lake that was only accessible by boat. You could soak in steaming pools of healing mineral water and dive into the icy lake to cool off.

It was the middle of July, the heart of a New Zealand winter. I had dropped in at about 2 p.m. to see if Janet's move into the cottage had gone well.

"Look at how stunning the lake looks. Not a breath of wind. I have found the motor and some gas for the dinghy. Let's go to the hot pools!" Janet suggested gleefully.

I agreed that a hot soak would be lovely and set about looking for the oars and life jackets.

"I haven't seen any. They must be locked up in his cupboard," Janet said.

"I could ask my friend up the road if we could borrow hers," I suggested.

"Nah, we'll be alright. Look how calm it is. Let's make the most of the afternoon," Janet said enthusiastically.

"Yeah, sure," I agreed. "We can just go along the shoreline."

The lake did not feel expansive like the ocean and felt deceptively safe when so calm. Rugged up in our jackets for the winter chill, we soon had the motor going and puttered our way slowly along the coastline in the small dinghy. The afternoon light sparkled warmly on the water. It felt gorgeous to be out on the water with the hot pools calling their welcome as we laughed and chatted. We crossed the lake at the narrow part of the channel and continued down the far shoreline to the pools.

"Ahhh . . . heaven," I sighed as I sunk up to my neck in hot water.

We had pulled the dinghy up on the sand and were the only visitors to the pools. It felt glorious to have them all to ourselves. We moved about the different pools of varying temperature and when overheated, I attempted my stride and plunge routine into the lake. By the time I got to the lake edge, I had already cooled considerably and a quick walk up to my thighs and out again was all I could manage. The water was icy.

I had read in the local paper that the lakes were so cold that you would expect signs of hypothermia if submerged for ten minutes. It was hard to even imagine a full ten minutes in that temperature!

The sun had begun its descent, so we decided it was time to head back. It was too dangerous to cross the lake back to the cottage without lights as we could be hit by a fisherman's speed boat.

As we set off up the coast on the mirrored surface of the lake, Janet pointed to a little bay on the other side of the lake.

"What's over there?"

I decided in a split second to alter our course and cross early at this widest section of the lake to show Janet the little bays with cute holiday cottages. We would then work our way back up that coast to Janet's new home. I opened up the throttle and the wee boat took off skimming effortlessly across the water. We were about half way across when I lifted my hand off the throttle to scratch an itch on the side of my nose. Every dinghy I had ever driven would hold its course whether you held the tiller or not, but this boat had a dangerously oversized motor. There was way too much torque for the weight of the boat and the propeller slammed hard across to the right, which turned the boat so suddenly that the bow was thrown straight up in the air. As if in slow motion, the stern submerged and Janet and I gently slid effortlessly into the lake. I remember the feeling of utter disbelief as the bow came down and the dinghy was left floating upside down.

I gasped for air as the shock of the cold water covered my body. Janet and I both instinctively held on to the hull of the dinghy. I saw two objects floating. One was a plastic-encased flashlight and the other a bailing scoop. I called to Janet to grab the flashlight as it floated past her and I had to swim away from the hull to get the bail. On returning to the upturned boat, the enormity of the seriousness of our situation became apparent to me. Our boat was upside down and we had no life jackets. Even if we righted the boat, we had no oars and how were we to get back in the boat? It would be dark within half an hour and there were no lights on in any of the holiday cottages as it was winter and they were not occupied.

To leave the boat to try and swim to shore would mean certain death. We were too far from either shore. It was at least a one-hour swim without cumbersome clothing, and hypothermia was ten minutes away, perhaps a maximum of fifteen minutes having raised our blood temperature in the hot pools. We had to get back in the boat. It was our only chance of survival.

"Are we going to be okay?" Janet asked me with an imploring look.

"Well, put it this way . . . we are in deep shit," I replied honestly.

I gave Janet the bail to hold and got under the side of the boat. With an almighty push I flipped the boat over. It was floating but full of water about six inches from the top. Janet in her panic, threw her body over the side of the semi submerged dinghy. This caused it to further fill with water and sink completely beneath the surface.

This was the only time I felt absolute fear. I thought the boat would sink to the bottom, and without life jackets in the unforgiving water we would surely die. As I watched for the inevitable gurgle as the boat silently sank, it just sat there, floating just under the water. I had no idea that these aluminum craft were built with floating baffles in the seats. Whoever came up with that good idea, I am eternally in your debt!

"We have to bail out the water, Janet."

I lifted the side of the boat while she began the task of emptying the boat of water. With one little scoop, it seemed an arduous task and progress was slow as I watched Janet struggling with the bulk of her jacket sleeve. I had only bought Janet the thickly padded jacket the week before. I had seen it in a secondhand shop while shopping with a friend. It was beautifully made, a big size and wonderfully warm to combat a Rotorua winter. She loved it and wore it all the time.

The bailing was too slow. We would never make it back in the boat in time.

"Here, throw it to me. I will have a go."

Bailing was awkward from the water, as my arm had to reach up and over the lip of the boat. My muscles quickly tired in this position. At least the boat was float-ing above water again but there was still the bulk of the water to shift. My upper arm muscle started to scream in protest with a burning heat. I considered throwing it back to Janet to rest my arm and for us to have turns, but I knew it would be too slow. I heard a soft whim-pering sound from Janet as she clung to her side of the boat white knuckled. I seemed to be maintaining body temperature through the activity of bailing but Janet was getting increasingly cold. Best to give her something to do, I decided.

"Hey, do you think you can push your side of the boat up. It makes it easier for me to reach the water. I'm going to get this boat empty and then we can get in it okay?"

Having some sort of plan seemed to jolly her along.

"I'm cold. Really cold," she shivered.

"Deep breaths and don't shut your eyes. Keep talking to me. You would think one bloody holiday maker could be at home, eh? They normally like to fish this time of year," I kept chatting.

I quickly realized that I could not bail and talk.

"How about you call for help as loud as you can. It is so still, your voice will carry a long way and you never know who might hear you," I suggested.

Task in hand, Janet regularly took a deep breath and called across the lake. In the meantime my arm was threatening to seize up altogether. With searing pain and solid determination, I stated my prayer.

"All the light that has ever come through these hands in the healing of others, I need you now for the power and strength to bail this boat! So be it!"

In that instant I was bailing at twice the speed and never felt another moment of pain.

This was the first *miracle*.

With the boat empty I got Janet to hold the bow down while I somehow pulled myself up and over the stern, using the outboard motor to hold on to. I knew that I had to get in the boat first as I was the only one that had any hope of restarting the motor, although I did not like my chances after it had been submerged in the lake. If I could start the motor I could tow Janet in a matter of minutes to shore. The petrol was still hooked up but I had no idea if there was water in it or not. I hand pumped fuel into the motor and tried the pull start over and over again to no avail. I could not afford to waste any more time for I had to help Janet out of the freezing water. Her cries for help had changed to a weak pitiful sound, like she was exhausted and giving up.

The hardest moment in the whole ordeal was the realization that I could not help to pull Janet over the side of the dinghy without capsizing the boat again and we would both surely die. I cursed at my stupidity for agreeing to go out without oars. I could not row her to shore or use the oar to help lever her into the boat. All I could do was balance the boat as she tried to pull herself over the side. She tried again and again but her efforts were futile. If she couldn't get out of the water she would become delirious and just slip beneath the surface and there was nothing I could do about it. I would have to watch her drown. It was down to mere minutes before she lost all strength to help herself.

"You have to remove your jacket Janet. It is too heavy!"

"No I can't," she complained. "I am too cold."

"Janet, listen to me! You will die in this lake tonight if you do not remove your jacket!"

The last of the sunset was glowing brilliantly in the west sky as Janet fumbled with her buttons and zip.

"I can't feel my fingers," she exclaimed.

"Quick as you can," I encouraged.

As the zip came down, Janet squealed as if in pain as the cold water rushed in to any remaining warmth in her body. The large padded jacket had held a vacuum of warmth against her skin. Again she cried that she wanted to keep the jacket on but gingerly surrendered its sodden weight over the side of the boat.

"Try again. Push!" I insisted.

She would get up to about nipple height, and that was it before sinking back into the darkening water.

"Kick off your boots!"

"They're brand new!" she protested but obliged.

I had looked frantically for a rope, anything, to help pull her up. Time was up. Janet looked totally deflated, her eyes closing.

"It's too hard," she said weakly.

The jacket! I could use the jacket. I grabbed one sleeve of the jacket and told her to hold on to the other. This time when she pushed herself up I could pull her towards me.

"Okay, push up. Come on, we can do this!" I shouted.

Janet was like a dead weight with not enough of her body over the lip of the boat for my pulling to be of any use. I was losing her.

I did not consciously set about to make her laugh, but that is what I did, which brought her around to a level of alertness for a brief time.

"Those big knockers you carry about on your chest. You have to throw them over the edge of the boat. That's all the leverage we will need!"

Janet laughed hysterically as she threw her breasts over the edge of the boat with her next attempt. She hung over the side precariously.

"Don't slip back! Hold the sleeve tight," I said with a glimmer of hope.

I pulled with all my strength as she wriggled and squirmed. Her rib cage, then stomach, and finally her thighs slithered into the boat like a giant eel, cast full length over the seats exhausted and not moving.

"Quickly, sit up," I coaxed. "We have to get your jacket back on."

I became aware of the uncontrollable shaking in my hands as I zipped her jacket up. I had not realized how cold I was. When Janet's shaking began, they were violent uncontrollable lurches that threatened to throw her off her seat. Her body danced constantly before me with deep shivering and shuddering. I saw this as a good sign as the body tried to warm itself. I hugged her close to me, hoping that our combined body heat would steady her spasms.

We were not out of the woods yet. Thank goodness there was no wind, so we didn't have an added chill factor, but it also meant we were not moving toward shore any time soon. We were out of the water, but would we survive a night sopping wet with temperatures dropping to −1°C? We had been having morning frosts all week. I continued to call "Help!" into the dimming light.

One of our floating companions, the bail scoop, had saved our lives so far and now it was time for the flashlight to be of assistance. I had Janet flash the flashlight off and on towards the shore.

I felt sure I could make out a light high up on the ridge amidst the glow of the sunset and then I heard some noise. It sounded like it was coming from a boat shed at the foot of the ridge below the light. My heart leapt with the anticipation that someone had heard us.

Suddenly I heard the roar of a motor in the opposite direction on the far side of the lake. I could vaguely make out the shape of a jet boat. There was no way the driver could hear my calls over the sound of his throaty V8 engine. I looked at the bluish shade around Janet's lips and again I prayed.

"I call upon the light of God to bring me that boat. We are so cold! I need it and I need it now! So be it!"

Instantly, there was silence as the boat's motor cut.

This was the second *miracle*.

We called into the silence flashing the flashlight. The V8 engine quickly roared into life and I held my breath for a moment to see if he would continue on his way or head our way. I watched as the bow swung in our direction and I was ready to cry with relief. I was trying to rub warmth into Janet's back.

"We're okay. Everything is going to be alright," I comforted her.

To this day, the skipper thought we had just broken down and needed a tow home. In the dimming light, he did not see how wet and cold we were. It was too far back to the cottage and Janet needed warming fast. I pointed to the track that led up to my farmhouse, which was three minutes away. If Janet couldn't walk the track, I had a farm vehicle that I could drive down to collect her.

"What made you cut your motor?" I asked the owner of the jet boat as we pulled into my jetty.

He was big, grizzly sort of bloke that suited his loud, powerful fuel guzzler.

"I dunno. I just saw the sunset and thought I might just stop and enjoy it for a while," he said, rather bemused.

"Is that something you would normally do?" I wanted to know.

He scratched at the whiskers on his chin. "Nah . . . can't say it is really."

His face wrinkled with confusion as if he was silently questioning himself, 'Why *did* I stop?'

He waved us goodbye on my jetty, unenlightened as to how close to death we had come. I pulled the dinghy up onto the sand and Janet and I walked as swiftly as we could up the steep hill to assist us in getting warm.

Once in the house, I put Janet under a hot shower where she slowly turned like a rotisserie roast slowly thawing her frozen body. I built a fire and got it blazing as I swapped my back for front to the heat of the flames. Janet wrapped up warm in front of the fire, hot cocoa in hand whilst I emptied the last of the hot water in the cylinder thawing my fingers and toes. We sat wrapped in blankets with our chairs just about in the flames for many hours until we finally felt warm again.

We didn't really talk about our near-death experience. We both knew it had been a close call and we were both processing a degree of shock in our silence.

For about five days, I could not hold my grip to pick anything up. The muscles of my right forearm and shoulder just would not work after bailing the boat. Janet had severe bruising right down her chest and across her breasts.

The next morning, I talked to Janet about the two *miracles* I had experienced, and that I wanted to lay flowers on the site where we tipped out of the boat to give thanks for the spiritual assistance that helped to save our lives. I also knew that I needed to get back in the dinghy to avoid a possible long-term fear of the water.

We were told that the dinghy was known to be dangerous as the 25-hp motor was way too big for the weight of the boat. Another friend had used the boat and at a much lower speed had let go the tiller and been flung all over the boat as it spun in circles. I intended to hug the coast and putter at no more than 5 kilometers per hour with a firm grip on the tiller as I returned the boat to the cottage. Janet plucked up the courage and decided she would come too. We picked a huge bouquet of red and pink camellias.

The motor started straight away, having dried out overnight, and we journeyed slowly to the middle of the lake. I felt a shudder of remembrance and a new-found respect for the deep dark water. We floated our flowers and watched them for some time and I said my silent prayer of thanks.

I looked up to the ridge where I had seen a light. I learned later that an eighty-year-old woman who was a permanent resident had notified her son when she heard our calls. He had traveled the half hour from town and was just preparing his boat when the jet boat came to our aid. I felt gratitude for our backup savior that night and sent a card of thanks to the elderly woman and her son.

I returned the dinghy and Janet to her wee cottage. I blessed the boat for having its floating baffles. Any other dinghy and I would not be writing this story.

To this day, I still prefer dry land and will not go on boats that are unfamiliar to me or with inexperienced skippers.

For a long time I pondered whether my instant *miracles* that day occurred because of divine intervention or instant manifestation occurred because of my focused intention.

When I made the statement, "All the light that has ever come through these hands in the healing of others, I need you now for the power and strength to bail this boat! So be it!" this was not a plea for help from a place of weakness and desperation. This was a statement to the Universe that made a demand I expected to be filled. It was only by being pushed to the very limit of my endurance that this ancient knowing came through me. I felt all powerful and once I knew that the dinghy would not sink, I had no fear. At no point did I believe that I would die. There was a period of time that I feared for Janet's survival.

"I need that boat and I need it now!"

Instant silence.

The Bible speaks about how we have the power of God within us with the intention that we hold dominion over the Earth.

On the last day of creation, God said, "Let us make man in our image, in our likeness." (Genesis 1:26)

God formed man from the dust and gave him life by sharing His own breath. (Genesis 2:7)

Scripture says that "God is spirit" (John 4:24) and therefore exists without a body. Adam's body did mirror the life of God insofar as it was created in perfect health and was not subject to death.

The image of God refers to the immaterial part of man. It sets man apart from the animal world, fits him for the dominion God intended him to have over the earth (Genesis 1:28), and enables him to commune with his Maker.

If my thoughts had been ones of panic and doom, I believe we would have died that cold winter evening. Because I called with intention on the great source of energy that is not me individually any more than it is separate from me, it responded accordingly.

I have spent many years learning and understanding the "law of attraction" in this dimension and I have manifested many a dream or visualization. Before this day, there had always been the small hint of doubt as to exactly how things came about.

"Was it really the power of my thoughts, my intention, or did that happen because . . . ?"

As soon as there is any doubt, the ability to instantly manifest through intention becomes limited. I had just experienced absolute clarity of intention because my life depended on it.

In the same way I have worked for years in my healing practice with the knowledge that the healer was not me individually, that I was a conduit (if you like) for a universal energy that came through me. I called upon that, that which I call God, my I AM presence. "So be it!" The response was instant. I have never witnessed my intention manifest instantaneously before, which is the realm of *miracles*. My clarity of thought was not diluted by indecision, doubt, or ambivalence.

One *miracle* and I could wonder about coincidence or rationalize that my muscles were so numb I could not feel them, which is why I could continue to bail the boat, but two *miracles* with the boat stopping instantly and manifestation through intention was an undeniable truth. We really are that powerful.

Crisis is often referred to as a "wake-up call" for this exact reason. This was my wake-up call. Wake up to the great being that you really are in full co-creation with God. You can manifest anything. If you want a positive outcome, have positive thoughts. If you want chaos and pain in your life, just keep immersing yourself in the frequency of it; keep listening to the sad stories; let your emotions of anger, hate, and resentment run unchecked. Chaos and pain will follow. It is up to you. It always has been. You reside on the planet of free will where *miracles* occur due to the power and clarity of your intention.

∽ 19 ∽

The Depths of Lake Rotoiti:
42 Years Old

Teaching: Tupena (Ancestors)

It was my first night sleeping in my little cottage right beside Houmaitawhiti Marae. Unlike a lot of land taken illegally, this land had been retained in Maori ownership and leased to those wishing to use it.

I was asleep, but not fully, as my body rested, but my mind remained alert. What I call my "between worlds." I could hear the cat licking her coat as my spirit was guided under the deep dark waters of the lake.

I was startled as the first face appeared. A man with a full face moko (tattoo) greeted me with a brief nod of his head. Next, a woman with a kauae (chin tattoo especially for women) gave me a broad smile. A kroua (old man) chuckled, a kuia (old woman) with long grey hair looked at me with love from deep brown liquid eyes.

"Tena koe," said a man about my dad's age.

I nodded in acknowledgement as face after face greeted me.

The cat continued her wash as I returned and became conscious of lying awake in bed. The wind howled and moaned the voices of the tupena (ancestors) from the past and I felt blessed by them.

I had been welcomed to my new home by those who walked the land many years before me.

⟫ 20 ⟫

Time for Sophia to "Cross Over":
44 Years

Teaching: Heaven

"Heaven: A place regarded in various religions as the abode of God and the angels, and of the good after death. A state of being eternally in the presence of God after death. A place, state, or experience of supreme bliss." (Oxford Dictionary)

At nineteen years old, darling Sophia had been through eleven house moves with me. Some called her a Himalayan Color Point, others a fluffy Seal Point with her cute chocolate face, ears, and feet.

My mother and I had gone to choose a cat for my Grandmother and wee Sophia was the tiny runt of the litter, all shy and quiet while the other kittens rolled and played. I could not leave her behind, so we came away with two kittens that day.

Sophia was particularly beautiful and had a gentle elegance about her all of her life. I was going to name her Sita or some such thing, and a friend of mine exclaimed, "She is way too posh for that. She should be named after a movie star!"

Hence, she was named after Sophia Loren.

The vet was always astounded at her robust health and ripe old age.

"These highly bred cats very rarely live past the age of ten years old," he had stated on various occasions.

Sophia proved them all wrong and stayed by my side. I adored her.

After a bad dose of cat flu in her youth, she would often get a repeat cough in winter.

"You can cut that out," I would say. "You're not going anywhere."

If she tried to get really sick by sitting out in the rain (usually because I had been away somewhere too long), onto the healing table she would go with a whole new meaning to "getting fluffed." This is what some of my clients called their energy sessions with me. Sophia loved it. She would lie stretched out with her eyes closed with a goofy smile on her face, paws twitching as she felt the energy from my hands above her body. I would make sure all systems were go with chakras spinning, turn off the relaxation music, and say, "There you go. That will do you."

She would open one eye to peek, "Are you sure that's all? Are you sure I don't need a little more fluffing. Purr . . . please?"

I would swoop her up onto my shoulder. "Come on you."

After Sophia's nineteenth birthday, she began losing weight and her kidneys were failing. We would talk about it.

"You know it will be that time soon, Sophia. You can go off and do it alone or let me know if you want my help. There is no need for you to experience any pain."

I had a trip away overseas for a month coming up and I was very aware that I had promised to help Sophia. I did not think she had that long to go, but she still had a good appetite and purred while bathing in the sunshine. It was just too soon.

"Sophie," I spoke to her one morning.

She couldn't be bothered lifting her head to look at me.

"Hey! This is important Soph."

She slowly rolled over, her big eyes focused on mine.

"I leave in ten days, that's ten sleeps . . .or make that forty-one in your case. Ten days Sophia. You have to let me know if you want my help to die."

The days went by and the morning before my departure I walked out of by bedroom to be met by Sophie sitting on the carpet staring at me. Once I had stopped and given her the attention she asked for, she stood up and then lowered her bottom into a full squat, as if to pee. She never messed inside, but she was old. I went to leap at her, like you would with a kitten and rush her to the door but I stopped as Sophie stood aside and showed me a tiny pee the size of a ten-cent piece. Her kidneys had all but failed, and she was letting me know it was time.

We cuddled a lot that morning and I cried. I made an appointment with the vet for the following morning and I gave that last day to Sophia. I found all sorts of treats in the pantry for her; John West wild salmon, ham, and fillet steak. She nibbled on bits and pieces, but was not very hungry. We lay on the lawn in the sun and talked about other worlds that were even more beautiful than Earth because the people had only love in their hearts. A place where there was only kindness, especially for beautiful movie stars. A place where I would see her again.

That night on her favorite mohair blanket, she sat on her chair and I on mine in front of the fire. I closed my eyes and in my mind I spoke with those through the veil in the fifth dimension where Sophia would be going. I requested that they guide her and take care of her until I saw her again. I then started to list all the things they needed to prepare for her.

"Her favorite game is to chase dry leaves in the wind, her coat ruffling deliciously in the breeze. She has spent most of her life in the countryside, so she will need wide open spaces and lots of sun. Her favorite blanket is pink and fluffy mohair."

With eyes closed, the tears were rolling silently down my cheeks as I processed saying goodbye to my loyal friend. It was hard to imagine life without her.

Suddenly I saw a bright white vertical tunnel of light.

'Wow,' I thought. 'That's like the tunnel people talk about when they return from a 'near death' experience. It must be coming for Sophia. I wonder if she will die tonight before I take her to the vet?'

The light came closer and closer, brighter and brighter, until it was right over the top of me. I was *in the tunnel*.

'Hey! I better not be dying,' I thought with sudden alarm.

Now I was floating, up, up, *up through the tunnel*.

"Oh man! I'm having one of those extra sensory, extra spiritual . . . extra terrestrial . . . extra experiences again, aren't I?"

If I had ever learnt anything, it was to relax.

"Don't fight it. Just let it be. If it is you dying tonight, so be it."

The more I relaxed, the more I floated until I had the feeling of popping out the top of the bright white tunnel. There before me was the most beautiful valley filled with yellow buttercups and rolling green hills. There was

Sophie in her young body on a farm track covered in big dry oak leaves. She was running to chase them, batting at them with both paws. Some distance away a woman walked. I could only see the back of her.

"Come on Sophia," she called.

Sophia sprinted to catch up to her.

Wham! I was back on the couch. My eyes opened and there was my Sophie sitting up, staring at me, her bright blue eyes, round like saucers.

"Sophie!" I exclaimed. "I have seen where you are going and it is beautiful! You must not be afraid to die. You will love it. I saw you in your young kitten body running really fast and there is a nice lady to look after you."

I picked her up and cuddled her old frail body in my arms. Because of all her fluff, Sophie still looked healthy and beautiful but she was as light as a feather. I snuggled my nose into the side of her cheek and spoke softly to her, "I will never forget the look of that valley Sophie. It is full of the most beautiful yellow buttercups. When I cross over I will go there to find you."

The next morning I sat Sophie on the front seat of the car wrapped in her mohair. She was a cat that had always yowled loudly in a motor car. When I transported her from Warkworth to our new home at Lake Rotoiti she yowled constantly with no let up for four hours.

On this day, she did not make a sound. She was alert and knowing.

From the car to the vet's clinic room, I held her to me and chatted to her about yellow buttercups. I held the paw that the vet shaved for the small plastic butterfly. She did not make a sound of protest as the needle went in. He drew up a small syringe of blue liquid, paused, and said, "Ready?"

I continued to look at Sophie. She had not taken her gaze away from me since we left the car. She was so still and calm. I kissed her forehead and squeezed her gently.

"Yes, we are ready."

It was eight years later that a visiting Swami from India said to me, "When an animal dies looking into the eyes of a human, it is ready to progress as a co-creator with God in human form."

I like to think of my beautiful, elegant Sophia enjoying her first human life somewhere in the world where there is still love and kindness in people's hearts.

At death, we leave this Earthly body of three-dimensional density and move with a lighter, more translucent body into the higher frequency of fourth- and fifth-dimensional energy. We are no longer in a place of duality; love and hate, good and evil. Without destructive thought, there is no disease process or decay. We reside in a light body that does not age and is forever youthful. We keep this light body until we rise to higher dimensions still, sixth and seventh, where this body resembling our Earthly body is no longer necessary.

The Great Experiment was to incarnate into the density of physical matter to be co-creators with God, the source energy in all manifestation including ourselves, so that we might fully experience our creations with the five senses of physical form; to touch, smell, hear, see, and taste. We incarnated with the Violet Flame of God Perfection, which resides in the human heart.

The original plan when entering physical form was to draw from universal light substances any form we desired through the power of the flame. We were never meant to be in a place of struggle and hardship nor forget the great beings we are. Our feelings energized thought forms and manifestation took place instantly.

When mankind no longer rested his attention on the God presence, but more on human creation, the Violet Flame became severely reduced in size, and our ability to co-create with God became increasingly limited. As we invoke and acknowledge God within us, our permanent self that never dies, we fill with light; our perfection expanding.

The Violet Flame is the great eraser of imperfect energy that is registered in the physical, mental, and emotional bodies, causing suffering and disease. They can be set free through the use of the Violet Flame. This is God's "Law of Grace" in action. The Violet Flame seizes imperfect energy and transmutes it so that it may be charged with perfection. The action is love, mercy, and compassion, which can dissolve the causes of distress.

What is referred to as the four lower bodies are the Mental, the Emotional, the Etheric, and the Physical. Only by cleansing the four lower bodies through the use of the Violet Flame can mankind attain mastery in the victory of his ascension into the light.

For many millions of years, we resided in physical form without duality of thought. With only loving, constructive thoughts, our bodies did not age and decay. The average lifetime was nine hundred years old, whereby we mastered all we needed to and then ascended (taking our body with us) into the higher frequencies once again of the spiritual realm.

When mankind in the third-dimension of free will "tasted the forbidden fruit" of duality and moved away from purity of thought represented by the feminine

(Eve), all of the undesirable experiences we know of in our Earth's history began to happen. Once people were capable of revenge, resentment, punishment, and power over others, they collected more and more karmic debt, in that they then had to experience what they had created.

". . . whatsoever a man soweth, that shall he also reap." (Galatians 6:7)

This has kept people in a constant cycle of birth, disease, and dying in very short lifetimes without mastering their lessons to achieve ascension. To add to this, the memory blank given by highly evolved beings to enable a fresh start, now has the human race with no memory of their past, who they are or where they have come from as great beings of light created by God.

In recent energy shifts on our planet, karmic debt has been erased and on mass we can now gravitate back to greater consciousness.

We are receiving amazing spiritual support, with many, many "light beings" from higher dimensions arriving on Earth, to remind people of who they are and we will see rapid changes from now on as Earth herself progresses toward a higher frequency of fifth-dimensional energy.

I am blessed to have experienced the tunnel of light and to have seen a place where the higher realm of heaven exists.

Jesus said, "In my Father's house are many mansions: if it were not so, I would have told you. I go to prepare a place for you." (John 14:2)

Heaven is the place we create with the power of our minds and our emotions. It is no different to how we are capable of manifesting on Earth; it is simply instantaneous in a higher frequency of fifth- or sixth-dimensional

Close to Death, Closer to God

energy. As I visualized the perfect heaven for Sophie to go to, it was instantly prepared for her.

I felt sudden sadness for all the souls who believed that there was nothing for them when they died, and by the laws of manifestation, they would arrive to a vast nothingness. This is not to say that there would not be guides willing to teach them and assist them to know differently, but the staunch and the stubborn determined to be right could drift in a sea of nothingness for a long time, or worse. If they believed they were truly worthless, guilty sinners, they may have imagined a fiery hell.

As we allow ourselves to imagine our life in a higher frequency exactly how we want it to be, in every detail with all the loved ones we wish to reunite with . . . so it is.

⌒ 21 ⌒

Ramtha's School of Enlightenment: 47 Years Old

Teaching: Discipline

I journeyed to Ramtha's School of Enlightenment, inland from Sydney, Australia. It is a school particularly focused on reminding you that God's wisdom is within each of us. Through breathing techniques, we could raise the frequency of energy in our bodies and we became capable of things we previously believed were not possible. All of the things we practiced involved *discipline*. With intense focus, we knew what the playing card was before turning it over. I have to admit, this was pretty advanced and not many were capable of it. I surprised myself by getting an almost 100 percent correct score in knowing whether the card was red or black. It was a combination of switching off the logical brain that said it was not possible and relaxing into the fact that my God intelligence, all knowing within me, already knew.

We practiced in pairs really studying the other person's facial features. We then sat on opposite sides of the room and held that focus without distraction. We took turns at sending each other an image while the other received it telepathically. I had the experience of receiving my partner's first image when I was supposed to be receiving the second image. It was like there was a small time delay. I was excited! He was told to send me any image at all and I received it. It was one circle drawn within another circle and I drew it exactly to size. As people succeeded in their sending and receiving, the pairs of pictures were pinned to the wall. There were hundreds of them. Someone had drawn a red rose with a green stem and one thorn and the receiver had drawn it exactly from one hundred feet away. I was impressed.

One of the most challenging tests was called "The Field." Five hundred students drew two pictures of things we would like to manifest. People drew houses, cars, piles of money, relationships, and families. One of my cards was a blue stick figure representing me with this radiant blue light all around me. It was me in my "Blue Body," which is me fully attuned with spirit in absolute consciousness.

The Field was fully fenced and all the cards, one thousand in total, were hung in bags all around the fence line. They had big flaps so there was no way that you could see the picture. All five hundred students entered The Field and put on blindfolds. We had to turn around and around until we had no idea which direction we were headed. We then had to walk in the pitch blackness.

The teaching from the Master was that when you were able to maintain the *discipline of no distraction*, you would walk untouched directly to your card.

"Yeah, right!" the logical mind sneers. Five hundred people locked into a pen like dodgem cars and one thousand pictures! Of course the logical mind sneers because logic is not capable of this task. Only divine wisdom could achieve this.

I quickly realized that The Field was representative of society with all its various personalities and distractions.

As people failed to hold their focus, they were constantly banged into or stepped upon and people responded in different ways to this. There were those who wanted to control the situation and have greater order in the field.

"No one should be allowed to wear boots in The Field!"

"You should not be allowed to walk swiftly in The Field!"

There were those that were afraid of the field. Afraid of confrontation. Afraid of pain.

There were others who just gave up and left The Field, and there were those who fell victim to the field as they got knocked over again and again until they retreated into tears exclaiming how unfair The Field was.

There were those who swore with rage that someone had collided with them while others burned with frustration for they could hardly say, "Watch where you are going!"

People hit the fence over and over again, only to check the card in front of them, see that it was not theirs, replace their blindfold, and head back into the throng of dusty sweating bodies.

I found myself distracted as soon as I heard the hurt cries of another. My mind would spontaneously say, "Is she okay?" and Bam! Someone would whack into my shoulder.

My mind would stray to my partner Manu. She walked with a stick after spinal surgery and had trouble keeping her balance without the blindfold, the uneven ground, and people banging into her. I had real concerns for her safety. . . . Ouch! Someone would stand on my foot. I saw my own pattern in society quite quickly as I observed myself becoming quietly annoyed that people were in my space. I lived remotely with hundreds of acres around me and no people, so all these people en masse barging into my space was a real challenge for me. After about ten minutes of regular battering I finally got it, that I could not fix it for all those that were suffering and there was nothing I could do to assist Manu. I was here to master *discipline*. The Field was representative of the world and I was learning how not to lose focus on my goal amidst chaos.

I stilled my mind and made the decision to only see my picture. I spoke to guidance and said, "If I am on the right track with this, give me a sign."

I was not convinced that the goal we had been set could actually be achieved. I needed something to give me a little faith, for all I could hear were cries of pain and frustration as people failed miserably.

The Master had said when our focus was improving, you will find a card very *like* yours, but it is not yours. It may be asking for the same thing or look very similar, thus it carries a similar frequency.

I hit the fence and lifted the flap in front of me. There was a Blue Body stick figure just like mine. The card had been placed in its slot upside-down, so it looked rather comical hanging with its head down. It was not my card, but very similar. It had a big letter "C" beside it, like, "See?"

"Okay, I will take that as a sign," I giggled with amusement. I was on to it now. I was focused. Within another few minutes I found my card.

At this point I knew I wanted to check on Manu. I saw her sitting out on the road in our rental car.

"Look, honey," I called. "I found one of my cards."

As I got closer, I could see that she was looking all bedraggled with dry grass in her hair and on her clothes.

"Oh, honey, are you okay?" I said with concern.

"I hate The Field," she said, her bottom lip quivering.

Poor darling had fallen over a number of times and people had stopped to help her up.

"What can I get you? What do you need?" I said with real compassion.

"I want a cake," she said sounding somewhere about the age of four years old.

I laughed to myself, having noticed the various reactions to The Field all afternoon.

"Then cake you shall have!" I declared.

I drove to the nearest bakery where there were about twelve different types of small cakes and I bought Manu one of each. It was a gesture of abundance.

"You can have anything that you focus on!"

We went back to the lovely apartment we had rented and talked about the day. Our energy was so raised that neither of us had any desire for any of the cakes. We ate not one and eventually they were thrown out.

In support of Manu, we stayed away from The Field for the rest of the week, however, I had a little "niggle" in my mind. What if getting my card was a fluke? Beginner's luck? I needed to know that the teaching was the truth, that with *disciplined focus* we can manifest anything, because it is the God force within us that is all-knowing and limitless.

I told Manu the next day that I had to return to The Field before leaving for New Zealand. I had to be sure.

I walked into The Field with the group of five hundred. I now understood that without disciplined focus, I was at the mercy of circumstance. I quietly coached myself, "If anyone can do this, you can. There is nothing else but your intense desire to be attuned to spirit, consciousness. Radiant in your Blue Body."

I finished spinning, eyes blindfolded in blackness and I walked. I was aware of the gentle whoosh of air as someone passed me but did not touch me. I kept walking, seeing my picture, seeing my awakened body, radiant in blue. I had the realization, "No one is touching me!"

I hit the fence for the first time after thirty seconds in The Field, lifted the flap, and there was my card.

My mind still wanted to say, "I don't believe it!"

"Believe it, believe it. You asked for proof of the teachings."

I remembered our teacher's voice. "You will walk effortlessly untouched directly to your card."

I had people coming up to me for the rest of that day.

"Thirty seconds! I have been coming here for years and I have never found my card!"

Comparing yourself to another, I observed, was yet another distraction.

It was not *me* that found the card. It was the energy that is in me, that is in every one of us, that is all knowing that could effortlessly walk directly to the card. As soon as the *me*, the small ego self with its mind full of clutter and distraction was no longer present, my great limitless *God self* knew exactly where my card was. It is the law of attraction in this dimension. As my mind stilled with *disciplined* thought to only hold my goal represented by the image on my card, my goal, the card, and my physical body were joined. This is the key to all manifestation. *With disciplined focus, I become the energy frequency of that which I wish to manifest, and it is so.*

I am so grateful for this experience to discover first-hand that with *disciplined thought* we can tap into God's wisdom, which is in each of us.

⁓ 22 ⁓

The Bull: 50 Years Old

Teaching: Trauma

I missed the bus, nan. Waka our moko (granddaughter) stood sheepishly beside my bed. Ahhh . . . just when I intended on getting a bit of a lie in.

"Why do you cut it so fine? Being more organized by five minutes would completely change my day!" I growled.

I had to move fast if we were to catch that bus. I would be more than growling if I had to drive the forty-five-minute return trip to the High School. This is not how I intended to start my day. I quickly pulled up trousers, not bothering with underwear, sweatshirt over the head, grabbed car keys, and ran out the door.

As I floored the accelerator down the winding country road, I saw a very large bull sitting on the side of the road. He is tan colored with a broad white face. As we pass him, he slowly turns his head, holding my gaze. His eyes are wild and unsettled, and he looks a bit mangy, breathing heavily with his nostrils frothing and discharging a ghastly looking mucous. He is not underweight, just tired as if he has been on the run for a while. Being naturally a herd animal, he would be unsettled roaming on his own.

"There is something not right with that bull," I think to myself.

I made a mental note to call Animal Control at the Council. It was always a danger to motorists to have stock loose on the road. We eventually caught up with the bus as it did the rounds picking up children at various stops. By the time I returned home, the bull was nowhere to be seen, so I gathered the farmer must have retrieved it.

Later the same morning, one of the older grandchildren and her young son came to visit.

"Hey nan, there is a cow in your driveway," she stated.

"Is it a tan color with a white face?"

"Yes, she is eating the grass in the gully."

"That's no cow. It's a stray bull. I will have to get it into one of our paddocks until I track down the owner."

I got busy with other things and didn't give it another thought until about 4 p.m. when I looked out the window. There was that massive bull in the house garden pulling at the shrubs.

"Oh, no you don't!" I exclaimed.

I quickly hatched a plan and opened a gate into my top paddock. As soon as he saw it, he would surely run for the long grass. He was on the lawn separated from the drive by a three-foot stone wall. Once he jumped down, he would see the open gate. I grabbed my stick and in a rather fearless gung-ho fashion I entered the driveway.

"Ho, Ho . . .off you go now!"

The bull considers his options to run back down the driveway, but in that moment he hears the voices of the children coming home from school. I manage to shout to the children to get off the driveway and get over the fence into the nearest paddock, as it may not be safe. I jump up the stone wall onto the lawn about 150 feet from the bull to encourage him to head for the open gate away from the children. He turns with a wild-eyed look and lowers his head. He is feeling trapped and does not want to jump the wall.

The last thought I remember is, "He's not going to stop."

The bull charges and his broad head with snotty nose hit me mid-abdomen. He tosses me at least three feet up into the air and off the side of the wall. I fall a total of eight feet and land heavily on my head on the unforgiving tar-sealed driveway. The bull is so enraged and fearful that he continues on through the garden and crashes straight through an eight-inch-thick post and rail fence, splintering the wood into many pieces. I am fortunate that once I am over the wall I am no longer in the bull's vision, so I am not pummeled or trampled further, which is common in such attacks.

I have a three-day hospital stay to deal with my head injury and the bull is dealt with by a neighboring farmer and eventually sold.

What stays with me from this experience is the knowledge that I have no memory of the incident once the bull looks at me and I know that he will charge. I did not see him begin to run in my direction or cover 150 feet of lawn. I have no memory of his head touching my body, nor had so much as a bruise where he made contact and lifted me right up off the ground. The only sign that he had been near me was the mess from his discharging nose smeared over my top and the small stones off the driveway in my hospital bed. I have no memory of flying through the air and falling at least eight feet to the ground, nor any memory of hitting the ground. How is that possible? Did I have the experience but the knock on my head blocked out all short-term memory or was it more likely that I left my body as soon as I knew the bull was coming in my direction? If I had stayed present, I could have easily jumped off the wall to avoid contact. The bull may have been mad enough or threatened enough by then to chase me off the wall where Manu was also standing. That scenario is definitely not worth thinking about.

During the process of my healing work to clear the etheric and emotional field, the client relaxes his or her body to trust again and various traumas become exposed for release. It is no different from clearing a blockage in the flow of the river, only to find that there are bigger boulders in the sludge that you did not know were there.

The work is not to have your client spend hours reliving or triggering trauma, but to acknowledge the trauma that is preventing the flow of life force and release the emotional response to it as quickly as possible. By clearing the field of such "clutter," not only does the client stop repeating similar traumatic events and emotions, but more of the purity of spirit can flow through the physical vehicle for greater health and spiritual awakening. This is an essential process for raising the frequency of energy in the body.

In all my years as a healer I had thought that the horror of physical or emotional pain resulted in the spirit disassociating from the trauma once the tolerance level was exceeded. This explained why children subjected to beatings or sexual abuse had pockets of memory, but often blocked all memory of the most traumatic events; however, my experience also showed me that the spirit could leave the body via the autonomic nervous system where there is no willpower or logical thought attached to the action. It could do this as a way of avoiding impending trauma.

You cannot remember something that you are not present for. The reality of what is happening is so terrifying that the spirit literally leaps away from the physical vehicle to the safety of the spirit world and returns when the event is over.

In my experience with the bull, one minute I am standing on the lawn, then my mind acknowledges what is about to happen, and then I am "gone" until I become conscious, lying on the hard driveway unable to move my head with my world spinning.

I did not need the actual *trauma* or physical pain of the event to cause me to leave my body. My spirit could depart my body without a decision or desire from my mind and could leave well before the event occurred.

☞ 23 ☜

The Pueo: 52 Years Old

Teaching: Feathered Messengers

I was up on the farm shifting stock a distance from the house. Three kereru (native wood pigeons) began to circle high overhead. I stopped to watch them, excited by their presence, as they were a rare sight. The undeniable "woo. . .sh, woo. . .sh" of their heavy wings became louder as they descended. I could see the white of their bellies and their magnificent green feathers on their breasts as they arced and turned. It was unusual to see them gliding in formation. They were often solitary birds with a specific flight pattern.

"Do you have a message for me?" I called silently to them.

The three birds descended rapidly and flew in circles above my head. The kereru brought *messages* to do with money and abundance. One would show itself if I was waiting on the payment of an invoice, and sure enough the money would be in the account by the next day.

I returned to the house and was joined outside by Manu.

"Money is on its way," I stated cheerfully.

"Great!" she responded.

"Not a small amount. A whole lot of money," I added. "There were three kereru."

I was bemused by this, as I had no inkling as to where a large sum would be coming from.

In that moment three kereru flew over the roof of the house swooping, dancing, and diving in front of us, putting on quite a display. This was complete confirmation that abundance was on its way.

The very next day, I had a call from a government department, requesting a meeting. One man in the department had managed to withhold funds owed to me for over ten years for fear of exposing his poor practice. After many requests for payment, which he successfully buried, it was finally exposed and the department informed me that I was due $85,000. After agreeing to accrued interest over the ten-year period, the settlement figure was closer to $200,000.

Many years ago a Maori kuia explained to me that in their culture they thought of the birds as "messengers from spirit." The piwakawaka (fantail) would fly inside the house when it had a message. Because it often brought the message from a loved one that had recently died, later generations mistakenly learned to see its presence as a bad omen of imminent death.

An Indian Swami confirmed many years later that birds were the most highly developed in the nature kingdom. They had evolved past being Earth- or oceanbound and had mastered flying. They were capable of moving as messengers between the heavens and the Earth.

Manu and I decided to consciously give various feathered friends individual tasks. The kereru was very large and fat, hence why it had been a popular food for Maori in earlier days. It overindulges on miro berries, stumbling drunk from its perch. For us, this represented more than enough or abundance, and so we gave it the task of allowing us to sight it when money was on its way. This was very useful in times when too little money was squeezed into too much creativity! The kereru is not a bird that we see a lot of, so when it appears to us in an obvious fashion it brings with it a clear message.

My name, Meryl, means blackbird. As a teenager, well before the teachings of the Maori kuia or the Indian Swami, I began to notice that when I was deep in contemplation asking what was the right action in any given situation, the blackbird would appear. The curtains could be closed with a small two-inch gap where they did not quite meet and the blackbird would appear perched on the wire outside looking directly at me through the small gap.

For a long time, I took minimal notice of such things and put their presence down to coincidence. The visits began to happen more frequently and always at a time, it seemed, when I was asking the questions, "Is this the right thing to do? Should I move in this direction?"

I would go to make a cup of tea and there on the post outside, six feet away, would be the blackbird always looking directly at me. I would be driving the car and one would dart out from the side of the road as they often do, but then fly incredibly close to my windshield or stop mid-air and flutter, which is most unusual behavior for a blackbird.

One morning, having sold my home in the north, I was waiting on the removal truck that would take me to the home I had built at Lake Rotoiti. It was a very big move with many challenges and unanswered questions as to what the future would hold. As I contemplated this, the blackbird flew into the garden, sat on an old tree stump outside my kitchen window and sang and sang. I gave thanks and journeyed with courage in my heart.

My Great Aunt also loved the birds and said, "The blackbird has one of the loveliest singing voices, but sings very rarely. A bit like you my dear."

When I think of the tui, it is known as the great mimicker. It can translate perfectly the sound it has learned. Manu, my partner, who relates to the tui can study anything and be teaching it with pinpoint accuracy by the next day. A great orator, just like the vocal tui. Her Maori name, Manu, translates as bird in English.

If you engage the assistance of the birds as messengers from spirit, then they will willingly oblige; if you do not, preferring to discredit this possibility, then they of course will not. A friend of mine was very skeptical about such things. One day we were sitting in her garden and I informed her that when Manu and I were apart, I had given the tui the job of bringing me messages from her.

"Yeah, right," my friend jeered with a laugh. "Well, seeing as she is away in the South Island, ask for the tui to visit now then," she challenged.

"Very well," I replied.

I focused on my love for Manu and with my mind called her to be with me through the presence of the tui. Not only that, I asked the tui to help awaken the consciousness of my friend.

Immediately three tui came into the garden and landed in a nearby tree.

"Hmmm, that is quite impressive, but not that unusual," her skepticism continued as she watched the playful tui.

"Take a look then," I said with a delighted smile.

High in the sky came at least ten tui! They swooped down and through the garden in perfect formation just like a squadron of tiny planes.

"Holy crap. . ." was all she managed as her mouth literally hung open, speechless of any further words.

She sat silently for quite a few moments, taking in what she had just seen. As if "coming to" she shuddered and got to her feet.

"You know, I hate it when you do that 'Hocus Pocus' stuff!! Holy shit!"

Holy indeed.

She quickly lit a cigarette and strode around the lawn completely dumbfounded.

This same friend came across a kereru with a broken wing. She phoned Manu to ask if she could eat it as she was a great hunter and gatherer and had always wanted to taste one. Manu's eyes lit up for a moment at the thought of such a delicacy.

"Tell her no, she can't eat it," I pipe up. "She needs to take it to the bird sanctuary. She will be rewarded with abundance for saving its life."

A week later her lotto ticket returned $800.

The day Manu and I met, she was with a committee of three other women and we sat for our meeting on Waimarama's headland overlooking Lake Rotoiti. The kahu (hawk) flew past majestically, gliding with its wide wingspan. I had been living away from the farm for a couple of years in a small cottage three kilometers down the road.

"I miss the kahu where I am living," I told them. "It lives here in the forest and does not come down as far as the bay. It used to fly past my bedroom window every morning to say good morning."

We completed our meeting and Manu suggested they come to my cottage for a coffee.

On my sun deck, the four women stood and sang a wiata (song) in my honor, for all the work I had done on the land preparing it to be a Healing and Education Centre. As the song began, I watched with amazement the kahu flying into the far side of the bay. In the three years I had lived there, I had never seen it. It not only circled through the bay, but flew slowly, wings outstretched in behind the four women about fifteen feet away. It had a beautiful speckled belly with white tips on its wings and was so close I felt as though I could reach out and touch it. Every hair on the back of my neck stood up and I knew something auspicious was happening that day.

For Maori, the kahu represents protection under its great wingspan. From that day on, I was no longer on the journey alone. Manu and I would love and protect each other. The kahu is particularly present when we are traveling. We can be in a queue of traffic and it will swoop low over the bonnet of our car only. On a number of occasions, it has appeared flying right beside my driver's window, turning its head to engage me with its beady eyes. He brings the message that we are divinely protected on the road.

We acknowledge the Piwakawaka as the one that carries the spirit of one recently passed before they cross over into the world of spirit.

One of my clients, Lisa, was diagnosed with leukemia and was told by her oncologist that she had three months left to live. After embarking on a wondrous spiritual journey, which involved many of my treatments, her body was dying eight years later. She had no partner and no children. We had a strong bond and Lisa asked to be near me as she faced death.

I set her up in my guest room on the ground floor, which received all-day sun and had a lovely view into the orchard. I took her delectable small servings of food and kept her pain free with the right doses of morphine. The plan was for her to stay as long as possible and then go to her sister's to die. Lisa just loved her time in the sanctuary of my one-acre garden, and after exactly seven days, her sister came to collect her. As I said my final farewell to my friend, I cuddled her fragile, painfully thin frame.

"Just one more week," she whispered. "I would love to stay one more week."

Three days later, I came downstairs and rolled open the sliding doors. It was summer and there was heat in the day already. As I made my morning cup of tea the piwakawaka flew into the house and fluttered through the living and dining rooms.

Lisa had died. I phoned her sister and she had taken her last breath at 5 a.m. that morning.

When I returned from the phone, I thought the piwakawaka was gone. I walked through the house and to my surprise it was sitting perched high up in the bookshelf.

"Hello there," I chatted away to the wee bird.

It chirped and jumped from left to right, fanning its tail happily. I left a nearby window open and one of the sliding doors and then spent some quiet time in Lisa's room where I said my prayers of farewell to her while she prepared to cross over. Later in the day I noticed the wee piwakawaka had settled down into a ball of fluff and did not appear to be leaving. I put a saucer of water on the shelf beside it and left the house for the day.

Later that night, my feathered friend was still with me and I had to close the windows to the evening breeze. I moved a nearby chair to prevent my cat Sophia climbing up to the bookshelves. As soon as I was awake, I opened the windows and doors but still it refused to leave. By 10 a.m. I was leaving crumbs of bread and seeds on the shelf.

The piwakawaka stayed exactly seven nights.

"Just one more week," she had whispered.

My friend Pat lived in my house at this time and became aware of the teaching that birds were *messengers from spirit*. She was facing death herself ten years later and had isolated herself from many of her old friends in the years before she died as if in preparation for letting go. We had not spent time with each other the year before her passing. I visited her when she was dying and we made our peace and said our goodbyes.

After Pat's funeral, I chatted to her in spirit off and on during the three-hour drive home. When I arrived back at my cottage, it was cold and I went to the wood shed to collect firewood. As I stood a meter from the corner of the shed, the piwakawaka darted over my shoulder and fluttered in mid-air right in front of me. I knew immediately that it was a message from Pat. It was as if she wanted me to forget her hurtful behavior of the previous year and the hurtful behavior of friends that had little to do with her over the years yet had excluded me from all funeral proceedings. The wee piwakawaka chirped and chirped as it flapped its wings and fanned its tail before me.

"Thanks Pat. Thanks for coming to see me. I will always love you. Journey well my friend and see you on the other side."

Close to Death, Closer to God

The dancing piwakawaka was a lot more like the cheeky fun-loving Pat I choose to remember. Pat was letting me know that she was free from an Earth of cruel people she struggled to understand and was again happy and smiling, free of the pain in her body and her heart. The adorable little bird chirped and fluttered over my head, then was gone.

One of my most significant bird visitations was on the Hawai'ian island of Kauai.

I woke early to a glorious day with views over the Pacific Ocean as far as the eye could see. The horizon sparkled in the distance. I felt truly blessed sitting in a wonderfully spacious two-bedroom apartment and felt delighted at my continued ability to manifest great things into physical matter. I had seen the photograph of this apartment and said in my mind, "That is what I want."

It was three times more than what Manu and I intended to pay. My American agent had booked the exact apartment for me at the same price as a basic one-bedroom unit after letting me down on a previous booking. The timing was such that the apartment had recently sold and the owners were happy with whatever extra money they could receive before settlement. Some would call it good fortune. I called it Focus.

The reason that this manifestation appeared so miraculously was partially because it was initiated by love for a friend who was joining us. I wanted her to have the pleasure of her own room and a private bathroom without cost to herself.

When the focus of manifestation involves emotional enthusiasm or giving to another, the power behind the manifestation is magnified through the power of the heart.

Manu and I sat in the early morning light of our first day in paradise to meditate for a half hour or so. During the meditation while calling in the Great Masters, I called to the Hawai'ian ancestors to please join us. In the next moment there were rivers of tears flowing down my cheeks. I was crying a deep grief yet I knew that it was not mine. I had no choice but to let the grief come. At the end of our meditation, I said to Manu that the grief felt ancient and belonged to the ancestors of the Hawai'ian people. I did not think a lot more about it and we went about our day exploring the beautiful garden island of Kauai.

Later in the early evening, I sat out on the lanai, casting my eyes out to sea to see if I could spot a whale or some dolphins. Suddenly with a flutter of wings there sat a huge owl sitting on a post only ten feet from where I sat. I could barely believe my eyes or conceal my excitement as I motioned soundlessly to Manu to look! . . . Look!

The Hawai'ians do not call this bird owl or ruru as we do in New Zealand. It is the pueo. It sat for a full minute, its big round eyes never taking their gaze from me.

"Hello," I said. "How lovely that you have come to visit me."

The pueo then spread its wings and flew into the dimming light of the night sky.

"Wow, wow . . . how amazing!" I exclaimed excitedly.

I went straight to the Internet to read about the Hawai'ian native owl, the pueo. It was the subject of many myths and legends. The one that immediately revealed itself to me was about a young Hawai'ian hunter. He came across a nest of large eggs, which he gathered into his carry bag. The pueo returned to her empty nest calling for her babies. The young hunter, seeing her distress, returned all of the eggs to her nest. He then took the Pueo as his God and built a temple in her honor.

"On a more esoteric level, the pueo, with all its mysterious wisdom, a bird that flew over the islands well before the first Hawai'ians sailed in, is among the oldest physical manifestations of the Hawai'ian family protectors, the ancestral guardians, the aumakua. It was believed that after the death of an ancestor, the spirit could still protect and influence the remaining family acting through a body such as that of the Pueo." (Veronica S. Schweitzer)

As I read this, I felt a tingling down my spine. I remembered how I had called the ancestors in the morning and with gratitude thanked them for being in their beautiful country. I had experienced their deep grief and that night they had visited me through the body of the pueo as promised in the ancient legend.

Only a few days ago, I was visited by the New Zealand ruru (native owl). I was driving down our long, tree-lined driveway just at sunrise, having picked up Manu's daughter off the early bus. There were big physical changes ahead and I had been contemplating our various choices. The wise decision was to opt for financial freedom with my partner, which would allow spiritual and emotional freedom, but there were various questions in the way.

As I came over the first hill, I came to the place where I always slowed right down because of protruding tree roots, and there standing on the ground before me in the middle of the driveway, was the tiny ruru, which brought me to a complete stop. It is not a bird that spends time on the ground, and if I had been traveling at normal speed, I could easily have run it over. The wise ruru sat in the exact place where I would see her. The *message* was to choose the wise decision as freedom has more value than anything in material matter. By allowing ease, all else would come.

The other birds we have asked to bring specific messages are the karerea, the New Zealand falcon. It is seen very rarely, and flies exceptionally fast with pinpoint accuracy close to the Earth. If seen, it says, "Hold your focus exactly and move swiftly to your goal."

The kingfisher with its beautiful green feathers and long beak gives guidance too. "Stick to the point. Don't waver. Don't waffle."

I give thanks for our wondrous *messengers* from spirit.

~ 24 ~

Daily Miracles:
"A Work in Progress"

Teaching: Peace

I did not choose death to experience the *peace* of being closer to God. My journey required that I experience the peace of God within me, as me, while maintaining my physical form. It would require intense, absolute focus and required circumstances that literally forced me to pay attention in the moment with no distraction of past or future.

All other thoughts are of secondary importance when I am fully occupied, focusing on how to survive. The words *fully occupied* are the key. There is no room for insignificant thought when my present time demands my undivided attention.

It is not possible to know *peace* without stilling the mind. To still the mind in everyday consciousness is like trying to listen to an exquisite violin concerto on the floor of the stock exchange, unless of course you have achieved mastery. To achieve mastery, the practice of meditation is essential.

No one has achieved the state of enlightenment in third-dimensional energy without becoming closer to God by taking the journey within to quiet the mind in meditation.

As long as our thoughts constantly leap about without discipline, they create a degree of havoc in our world of manifestation. I may clearly ask for one thing, but then a following thought completely cancels it out.

As you were!

It is like writing creative sentences all day and constantly running over them with an eraser. Nothing happens!

The person who heals their life-threatening disease will need to fully focus on modifying thoughts, attitudes, diet, and other stress factors that contributed to their imbalance. I have heard the words hundreds of times, "If it were not for my diagnosis, I would never have begun this journey."

The journey speeds them on to greater physical health, emotional peace, and ultimate spiritual awakening that they would not have commenced without the kick start of their illness and the motivation to live.

If it were not for my apparent foolhardiness and the subsequent close shaves with death, I would not have awoken to my inner knowledge.

Deep reverent *peace* is only possible in a life of focus, without life-threatening drama or distracted thoughts leading to undisciplined emotion. A life filled with daily miracles. To even begin to succeed in this, the consciousness of *peace* must be with us daily; not just now and again when we think about it or read about it. If all manifestation first begins with thought, we must think about our inner peace *every* day and *many* times during the day as we invoke our mighty I AM presence.

When we begin the day with meditation, it teaches us present time focus, which allows a surrender of busy thought and bathes our being in the peace that resides within us. Even in the stillness of a specified meditation time, it takes great practice to become conscious of what the mind is doing and to learn how to observe thoughts. The mind is as "quick as a whip," and wants to wander off into thinking. One thought leads to another, which leads to another, creating chains of thoughts. The extreme of this state is to have no conscious knowledge of the thoughts as you enter the dream state and the body falls asleep. As we learn to observe thoughts, we are back in present time in that moment, and we get more efficient at simply releasing superfluous thoughts.

'Not now! I will give that more thought later,' or, 'No, those thoughts do not serve me in any way.'

It is important for us to recognize the destructive thoughts that we *want to hold on to*. These thoughts deny us peace. They are usually the thoughts that we have strong emotional attachment to, perhaps a sense of injustice that we want to think about over and over again. We enjoy gossiping about how we have been wronged, insisting that we are right or we just want to worry about something we fear in the future that hasn't happened yet.

In observing such thoughts honestly we can choose to place that thought in a bubble and watch it float away. Even if it is something that will require more thought at a later time to resolve, it requires the discipline of saying, "Not at this time!" if we are to know peace. We must decide that nothing is more important than mastering the journey to absolute peace, for peace is to know God.

When practicing this, it is so much easier for us to stay in present time if we meditate with a guide. The music and the voice brings us back into focus, where we are able to realize that our thoughts are wandering; in fact, without such assistance any real peace can evade us. We can relax our bodies, but our minds continue to chatter in thought or the dream state as we drift in and out of sleep.

True, blissful peace occurs when our brainwave pattern changes from Alpha (relaxation) to Theta, which occurs for most people as a momentarily state before entering the Delta brainwave of sleep. This is why many people find meditation so difficult. They feel that their efforts are futile or, in this busy world of *doing*, that it is a waste of their precious time. The strange irony is that to know *peace* is to be in the present moment where time does not exist.

With practice, letting go the chains of thoughts from one thought that creates another, we experience an extended time of Theta brainwaves. In this state, the body feels deeply asleep, but the mind is alert and *conscious* where we can experience *being, the I AM presence, that which is God*.

A great joy bubbles to the surface like laughter from the inside. You may see visions of color, hear guidance with clairaudience, and intuitively know spiritual truth.

There are millions of people at this time that are permanently cut off from the great, joyous beings they are capable of becoming, if they would only tune in to themselves. Like a poor radio connection, they are just off the station surrounded by static and needing to center the dial for clarity. They jump from one action to the next with barely a moment in between. When they have finished doing what they must achieve for the day, they jump into doing some form of entertainment, socializing, watching television, or becoming preoccupied with thoughts about past or future worries. Even reading a good novel can immerse them for hours in someone else's world. Their success or exceptional achievements are given only a moment of thought as they hurriedly move on to the new. There is no time for *gratitude*. The emotion of gratitude is like a spear of divine light that opens the heavens for blessings to rain upon us. It feeds the main crown chakra, increasing energy flow and vitality to our bodies and our emotional field, which directly assists our spiritual awakening.

Stopping the constant *doing* initially allows more emotions to surface. Being very busy is a great distraction from the anxiety of feeling more. When our mind agrees to *feel everything* and not be afraid of past pain or the hurt of current circumstances in our world, our hearts open further, which draws a higher frequency of light through our bodies, forging a direct path to *peace*.

A guided teaching meditation will continue to feed the mind with the logical thoughts of listening and understanding, which is not true meditation; however, it teaches the mind to slow down and focus its thoughtforms on more simple present-time tasks, training the practitioner to recognize when the mind is wandering. This is extremely useful until the mind no longer requires the prompts to achieve this.

Once in a peaceful state of *being*, we experience our completeness. Everything that is required for a happy and fulfilling life is within us. By looking outside of ourselves for happiness, our life will feel empty in comparison, except we will not know this until we know *peace*.

Without peace, we continue to seek change in our material world to fill the void in our search for completeness and in turn bring suffering upon ourselves.

The loneliness and depression that older people feel when there is less for them to do or their aging physical body demands that they accomplish less is directly attributed to their inability to *be*. Some make the transition easier than others as they teach themselves to simply be sill, observing a sunset, enjoying the change of seasons, or perhaps tending a garden. Most experience fear and panic when doing less, as it appears that their source of happiness is drying up.

To seek happiness and satisfaction from outside of the self—through other people, places, and events—is to see happiness as something separate from ourselves that we must obtain. We receive fleeting moments of happiness from these external sources, but they are like a mirage in the desert. In a moment of awe you see a beautiful diamond jeweled mansion, and then it evaporates into your marriage settlement, insolvency, or deceased estate. The illusion that happiness is something to seek outside of the self simply pushes happiness further away.

To fully understand the intense happiness of simply being, we have to understand the difference between inaction and non-action. Inaction is resistance and laziness. The non-action of discovering our own peaceful being only occurs when engaging the heart as an effortless, natural expression of being. To be busy *doing* in the hope of *being* is indeed back to front when peacefully *being* leads us to flow from a space that influences all that we *do*.

Finding peace is not an action, but a state of being. From the state of being, all creative action can flow with joy and ease.

Our aim is not to spend our life in meditation, but to allow our state of meditation to overlap our every waking moment so that peace is the foundation of all thought, speech, and action.

When we achieve this, we are directly contributing to the healing force that brings peace to our planet. One more person stops, takes a deep breath, and has a moment to *be.*

Our enlightened state is when we retain the ability to actively live in purity of all thoughts, speech, and actions. We then realize that there are many levels to our awakening with finer and finer frequencies of energy. When more than 50 percent of our being becomes the finer frequency of pure love, compassion, and grace, our ascension is possible. When more than 50 percent of the population experiences this state of being, the balance will tip and all beings on planet Earth will live in the higher frequency of fifth-dimensional *peace*. The body no longer dies and decays, but transforms the higher energy of light frequency into a solar light body that is in no way limited by time or space.

If you have ever spent time pondering how you can best assist this awakening on planet Earth, then know to begin with the self. Go within and become the higher frequency of love, and then project it out into the world. Many great teachers have attained this state, and every one of them would say, "I have continued on in my evolution, to attain an even finer frequency of infinite light and infinite love. Forever, a 'work in progress.'"

About the Author

Meryl Yvonne Crump was born in 1960 in the small city of Whangarei, Northland, New Zealand, the middle child of three girls. Her parents taught her the values of hard work and determined effort. Her carefree childhood gave her a connection to the land and a freedom of spirit.

Meryl entered High School at the age of 12 where she qualified for the First VI Hockey Team, and went on to be accepted for the Northland team. She began her career in nursing at 16 and graduated with Honors. She wrote and performed songs from 18 and at the age of 22 was recording in a Nashville studio and performing on New Zealand television. In 1984, she was awarded "Most promising female vocalist" at the New Zealand Music Awards.

Today, Meryl runs the Healing Center Waimarama with her partner Manu Neho. Her greatest passion is to assist people in taking the journey within, to find the bliss and peace that is their God given right to access. She has written this book which includes her own experiences to both entertain and share with the reader her spiritual truth that she has discovered on her own journey. Until the world is a place of peace and prosperity for all, her work continues.

Visit her online at:
www.waimarama-international.co.nz

Go to http://www.shop.waimarama-international.co.nz
for a FREE "Beginners Guide to Relaxation."

This is a quality production with the magical sounds of
traditional Maori musical instruments. It will assist you
to begin meditation or there are more advanced meditation recordings available to enhance your current
meditation practice. This book can also be ordered from
the website at a wholesale price and further discounts for
multiple orders.

Buy a set of meditation downloads and receive a free
copy of this book.

"Be the change you wish to see in the world."
(Mahatma Gandhi)

Please email feedback that may assist others. Include any
life-changing experiences that catapulted your spiritual
awakening to:

meryl@waimarama-international.co.nz

Look out for a Blog on the Waimarama web site. All
questions and contributions welcome in our mutual
pursuit of love and happiness for all.

www.ingramcontent.com/pod-product-compliance
Lightning Source LLC
Chambersburg PA
CBHW020607270326
41927CB00005B/210

* 9 7 8 1 6 1 8 5 2 0 8 6 9 *